Excellent English 1
Language Skills for Success

Susannah MacKay
Kristin D. Sherman

Jan Forstrom
Marta Pitt
Shirley Velasco

McGraw-Hill

Excellent English Student Book 1

Published by McGraw-Hill ESL/ELT, a business unit of The McGraw-Hill Companies, Inc.1221 Avenue of the Americas, New York, NY 10020. Copyright © 2008 by The McGraw-Hill Companies, Inc. All rights reserved. No part of this publication may be reproduced or distributed in any form or by any means, or stored in a database or retrieval system, without the prior written consent of The McGraw-Hill Companies, Inc., including, but not limited to, any network or other electronic storage or transmission, or broadcast for distance learning.

ISBN 13: 978-0-07-340644-2 (Student Book)
ISBN 10: 0-07-340644-9
1 2 3 4 5 6 7 8 9 10 QPD 11 10 09 08 07

ISBN 13: 978-0-07-719284-6 (Student Book With Audio Highlights)
ISBN 10: 0-07-719284-2
1 2 3 4 5 6 7 8 9 10 QPD 11 10 09 08 07

Series editor: Nancy Jordan
Developmental editors: Nancy Jordan, Eve Einselen
Cover designer: Witz End Design
Interior designer: NETS

The credits section for this book begins on page 222 is considered an extension of the copyright page.

McGraw-Hill

The *McGraw-Hill* Companies

Acknowledgements

The authors and publisher would like to thank the following individuals who reviewed the *Excellent English* program at various stages of development and whose comments, reviews, and field-testing were instrumental in helping us shape the series.

Tony Albert • Jewish Vocational Service; San Francisco, CA

Robert Breitbard • Collier County Adult Education; Naples, FL

Jeff Bright • McHenry County College; Crystal Lake, IL

Sherrie Carroll • Montgomery College; Conroe, TX

Georges Colin • Lindsey Hopkins Technical Education Center; Miami, FL

Irene Dennis • Palo Alto College; Palo Alto, CA

Terry Doyle • City College of San Francisco, Alemany Campus; San Francisco, CA

Rolly Fanton • San Diego City College; San Diego, CA

Colleen Fitzmaurice • San Diego Community College District, Mid-City; San Diego, CA

Phil Garfinkel • Adult & Family Education of Lutheran Medical Centers; Brooklyn, New York

Ana Maria Guaolayol • Miami-Dade College, Kendall Campus; Miami, FL

Margaret Hass • San Diego Community College District, Mid-City; San Diego, CA

Giang Hoang • Evans Community Adult School, Los Angeles Unified School District; Los Angeles, CA

Armenuhi Hovhannes • City College of San Francisco, Mission Campus; San Francisco, CA

Vivian Ikeda • City College of San Francisco, Teacher Resource Center; San Francisco, CA

Sally Ruth Jacobson • San Diego Community College District, Centre City; San Diego, CA

Kathleen Jimenez • Miami-Dade College Kendall Campus; Miami, FL

Nancy Johansen • San Diego Community College District, Mid-City; San Diego, CA

Mary Kapp • City College of San Francisco, Chinatown Campus; San Francisco, CA

Caryn Kovacs • Brookline Adult Education; Brookline, MA

Linda Kozin • San Diego Community College District, North City Center; San Diego, CA

Gretchen Lammers-Ghereben • Martinez Adult Education School; Martinez, CA

Paul Mayer • Glendale Community College; Glendale, CA

Lee Mosteller • San Diego Community College District, North City; San Diego, CA

Iliana Pena • Lindsey Hopkins Technical Education Center; Miami, FL

Howard Riddles • Tomlinson Adult Learning Center; St. Petersburg, FL

Lisa Roberson • Mission Language and Vocational School; San Francisco, CA

Renata Russo Watson • Harris County Department of Education; Harris County, Texas

Francisco Sanchez • Miami-Dade College, Kendall Campus; Miami, FL

Curt Sanford • City College of San Francisco, Alemany Campus; San Francisco, CA

Laurie Shapero • Miami-Dade College, Kendall Campus; Miami, FL

Eileen Spada • Max Hayes Adult School; Detroit, IL

Margaret Teske • Mt. San Antonio College; Walnut, CA

Theresa Warren • East Side Independence Adult Center; San Jose, CA

D. Banu Yaylali • Miami-Dade College, Kendall Campus; Miami, FL

Scope and Sequence

Unit	Grammar	Vocabulary	Listening/ Speaking/ Pronunciation	Reading	Writing
Pre-Unit *page 2*	• Parts of speech (nouns, verbs, adjectives, pronouns)	• Alphabet • Greetings • Numbers	• Follow classroom directions • Spell your name aloud	• Read sentences about school	• Write the names of your classmates
1 **All About You** *page 6*	• Simple present of be: Statements • Singular and plural nouns • Irregular plural nouns • Contractions • *a/an*	• Personal information • Countries • Occupations • Addresses	• Tell where people are from • Introduce yourself • Talk in a small group • Discuss occupations • Ask for and give personal information • **Pronunciation:** *Teens* vs. *ty's* (*fourteen* vs. *forty*) / Stress in numbers	• Read personal information forms • Read a personal letter • Identify capital letters in names	• Write about occupations • Complete forms • Write your name and address on an envelope • Use capital letters with: first names, streets, cities, the first letter of a sentence and salutations
2 **My Family** *page 22*	• *Yes/No* questions with simple present of *be* • Possessive adjectives • Possessives of nouns and adjectives • Subjective pronouns	• Personal characteristics • Physical appearance • Family members	• Describe physical appearance • Identify family members • Interpret a chart • Take and leave phone messages • **Pronunciation:** *Is he* vs. *Is she*	• Read about a family • Transcribe and read messages • Read a personal story • Use pictures to think about text	• Write about your family • Make a list to get ideas for writing
3 **At School** *page 38*	• *There is/There are* • Prepositions of location • Questions with *how many*	• Classroom objects • Classroom furniture • School supplies • Library facilities • Directions and signs	• Tell about classroom objects • Name school supplies • Ask about library facilities • Listen to a phone conversation • Describe locations at school • Ask for and give directions at school • **Pronunciation:** Stress in compound nouns	• Examine a map of a school • Read a sign • Collect information from a website • Take notes on a diagram	• Complete a sign with information • Use correct punctuation • Capitalize the first letter of a sentence • Use periods or question marks
4 **It's About Time** *page 54*	• *It's* with weather • Information questions (*what time, when*) with simple present of *be* • Prepositions of time (review)	• Weather words • Temperatures • Seasons • Months • Times • U.S. holidays • Ordinal numbers	• Describe weather and seasons • Listen to a weather report • Ask about and tell the time • Discuss holidays at work • **Pronunciation:** Ordinal numbers	• Read a pie chart • Read and understand a school calendar • Understand and write an email message • Locate important details before you read	• Write the time • Make a school calendar • Write about the weather

Civics/Lifeskills	Math	Critical Thinking	Correlations		
			CASAS Life Skill Competencies	SCANS Competencies	EFF Content Standards
• Follow directions	• Learn numbers 1-20	• Name the letters of the alphabet • Recognize numbers from 1-20	**1:** 0.1.1 **1:** 0.1.4 **1:** 0.1.5 **1:** 6.0.1	• Interpret and communicate information	• Listen actively • Speak so others can understand
• Address envelopes • Learn about community workers • Complete a school registration form • Read information from a Social Security card and employee badge	• Understand and pronounce numbers • Complete personal forms using numbers • Recognize patterns in forms	• Analyze information • Practice small talk • Relate to jobs	**1:** 0.2.1 **2:** 0.1.2 **3:** 0.1.4 **4:** 4.1.8 **5:** 0.1.2 **6:** 0.2.2 **7:** 0.2.3	• Acquire and evaluate information • Interprets and communicate information • Work with cultural diversity	• Convey ideas in writing • Resolve conflict and negotiate • Use math to solve problems and communicate • Learn through research
• Give and take a phone message • Have conversations at work	• Interpret a height chart • Say telephone numbers	• Describe yourself • List your ideas about a story • Compose a message • Review a telephone message	**1:** 0.1.2 **2:** 0.1.2, 0.1.4 **3:** 2.7.6 **4:** 0.1.4 **5:** 0.1.4, 6.6.1 **6:** 2.1.7, 2.1.8 **7:** 0.1.2, 0.2.4	• Understand systems • Apply technology to task • Participate as a member of a team	• Read with understanding • Convey ideas in writing • Cooperate with others • Reflect and evaluate
• Use library resources • Locate school facilities • Read a map to find places in a school	• Use multiplication to answer questions about classroom items • Locate room numbers in a building • Read enrollment and school statistics	• Identify classroom objects • Locate school facilities • Find your way around campus	**2:** 6.1.3 **3:** 2.1.8, 2.5.6 **4:** 2.2.1 **5:** 2.5.5 **6:** 2.5.4	• Organize and maintain information • Monitor and correct performance	• Speak so others can understand • Listen actively • Cooperate with others • Take responsibility for learning
• Communicate information about the weather • Listen to a weather report • Read a school schedule • Practice a conversation about school holidays	• Read a pie chart about the weather • Understand Celsius and Fahrenheit temperatures • Ask about and tell the time • Interpret a school calendar • Ordinal numbers Write dates	• Predict tomorrow's weather • Assess today's weather • Examine calendars • Compose schedules	**1:** 2.3.3, 5.7.3 **2:** 2.3.3 **3:** 1.1.5 **4:** 2.3.1 **5:** 2.3.2, 2.7.1 **6:** 2.5.5, 2.7.1 **7:** 0.2.3	• Interpret and communicate information • Understand systems	• Convey ideas in writing • Observe critically • Learn through research • Use information technology and communications

Civics/Lifeskills	Math	Critical Thinking	Correlations		
			CASAS Life Skill Competencies	SCANS Competencies	EFF Content Standards
• Describe people and places in the community • Follow directions to places around town	• Understand numbers on traffic signs • Calculate distance using a map	• Memorize traffic signs • Recall directions • Report an accident	1: 2.2.1 2: 2.5.1, 2.6.2 3: 2.5.3, 2.6.1 4: 2.2.1 5: 2.2.1, 2.2.2 6: 2.2.5 7: 2.5.1	• Teach others • Exercise leadership • Work with cultural diversity • Apply technology to task	• Read with understanding • Listen actively • Guide others • Use information technology and communications
• Choose the correct clothes for an occasion • Shop for clothes and accessories	• Identify U.S. coins and bills • Ask about prices • Write the price of items • Interpret a receipt • Write a personal check • Make a budget	• Select clothing styles • Evaluate quality • Choose size • Compare prices	1: 0.1.2 2: 0.1.2 3: 1.3.7, 1.3.9 4: 1.1.6 5: 1.2.1, 1.6.4 6: 1.2.1, 1.8.1 7: 1.2.1	• Allocate money • Acquire and evaluate information • Negotiate	• Read with understanding • Observe critically • Advocate and influence • Use math to solve problems and communicate
• Plan by scheduling • Calculate your pay according to your work schedule	• Use time for daily schedule • Compute hourly wages	• Apply job routines • Choose a schedule • Distinguish family and job routines • Answer questions about a pay stub	1: 0.2.4 2: 2.3.1, 2.3.2 3: 2.3.1 4: 0.2.1 5: 0.2.4 6: 4.2.1, 4.4.3 7: 0.2.4	• Allocate time • Allocate material and facility resources • Interpret and communicate information • Participate as a member of a team	• Listen actively • Solve problems and make decisions • Plan • Use math to solve problems and communicate
• Practice grocery shopping • Read and order from a menu • Prepare food for a business meeting	• Listen and write about food prices • Compare prices at the grocery store • Use weights and measurements in recipes	• Interpret unfamiliar foods • Calculate your share of lunch • Experiment with new menu items • Test a recipe • Judge quality and price of food	1: 1.3.8 2: 1.2.1, 1.3.8 3: 1.2.1, 1.3.8 4: 0.1.2 5: 0.1.2, 1.1.1 6: 1.2.2, 1.3.8 7: 2.7.2, 2.7.3	• Allocate time • Allocate material and facility resources • Organize and maintain information	• Speak so others can understand • Guide others • Take responsibility for learning • Reflect and evaluate

Unit	Grammar	Vocabulary	Listening/ Speaking/ Pronunciation	Reading	Writing
9 **Skills and Work** *page 134*	• Past tense statements • Regular past tense verbs • Irregular past tense verbs • *Can* for ability	• Job skills • Occupations • Parts of a pay stubs • Job advertisement abbreviations • Job application headings	• Talk about your abilities • Listen to descriptions of other people's jobs • Listen to a job interview • Practice job interviews • **Pronunciation:** *Can* vs. *can't*	• Read about jobs • Read a pay stub • Interpret job ads, understand the abbreviations • Use headings to find information	• Write about your abilities • Write about job skills • Fill out a job application • Edit important documents and forms
10 **Taking a Trip** *page 150*	• Simple past of *be*: Statements • Questions with the simple past of *be* • Adjectives	• Transportation (forms of) • Adjectives to describe travel • Travel problems • Recreation locations	• Talk about a trip • Talk about a bus schedule • Apologize for being late • Answer questions about yourself • Listen to an advertisement • Talk about advertisements • **Pronunciation:** Interjections	• Examine a bus schedule • Read an email • Read about a weather emergency • Use context to understand meaning	• Write about a vacation • Edit your writing for correct verb forms
11 **Health Matters** *page 166*	• *Should* for advice • Simple present of *have*	• Health problems • Parts of the body • Remedies • Health habits	• Describe people's feelings • Listen to telephone messages • Call in sick to work • Talk about health problems and remedies • Describe health problems to a doctor • **Pronunciation:** *Should/shouldn't*	• Read an appointment and an insurance card • Read about healthy habits • Use pictures to guess the meaning of new words	• Write a conversation you just heard • Write about health problems and remedies • Write advice for health problems • Indent a paragraph
12 **Planning ahead** *page 182*	• *Be going* to for future: Statements • Object Pronouns • Questions with *Be Going To*	• Life milestones • Furniture • Appliances • Rooms of a house • Household repairs and improvements	• Talk about your future plans • Communicate with a landlord • Extend an invitation • **Pronunciation:** *Gonna* (for *going to*)	• Read and understand housing ads • Read about the three steps to change • Look at a title before reading a passage	• Write a to do list • Write sentences about your plans • Use examples to make your writing interesting

Appendices

			Correlations		
Civics/Lifeskills	Math	Critical Thinking	CASAS Life Skill Competencies	SCANS Competencies	EFF Content Standards
• Read job ads • Complete a job application • Participate in an interview	• Interpret a pay stub • Read hourly pay	• Write a resume • Operate productively • Express employment related goals	**1:** 4.1.8 **2:** 4.1.8 **3:** 4.1.6 **4:** 4.6.4, 4.6.5 **5:** 4.2.1, 4.6.5 **6:** 4.1.3, 4.1.5 **7:** 4.1.2	• Allocate human resources • Serve clients or customers • Negotiate • Improve and design systems	• Speak so others can understand • Cooperate with others • Resolve conflict and negotiate • Reflect and evaluate
• Read an email • Interpret train schedules • Read vacation ads	• Understand a bus schedule • Understand a train schedule • Calculate travel times and cost using public transit	• Prepare according to train schedule • Arrange for emergencies • Compare fares • Schedule a vacation	**1:** 2.2.3 **2:** 0.1.2 **3:** 2.1.7, 4.6.4 **4:** 0.1.3, 0.2.4 **5:** 2.2.4 **6:** 0.2.1, 1.2.1 **7:** 2.3.3	• Allocate time • Allocate material and facility resources • Teach others • Improve and design systems	• Resolve conflict and negotiate • Solve problems and make decisions • Take responsibility for learning • Learn through research
• Read medicine labels • Complete a patient information form • Read appointment and insurance cards • Visit the doctor	• Understand time on an appointment card • Understand an insurance card	• Recognize symptoms • Classify diseases • Define good health habits	**1:** 3.1.1 **2:** 0.1.2, 3.1.1 **3:** 2.1.7, 2.1.8 **4:** 3.1.3 **5:** 1.4.1, 1.5.2 **6:** 1.4.2 **7:** 3.5.2, 3.5.5	• Allocate money • Organize and maintains information	• Observe critically • Guide others • Advocate and influence • Solve problems and make decisions
• Read housing ads • Plan for the future • Find housing in the community	• Interpret a calendar • Interpret a timeline • Add, subtract and divide numbers	• Discuss a rental lease • Explain timelines • Develop a floor plan	**1:** 0.1.2 **2:** 0.1.6, 7.1.4 **3:** 7.2.7 **4:** 1.4.1, 1.5.2 **5:** 1.4.1, 7.4.3 **6:** 1.4.2 **7:** 7.1.2, 7.1.4	• Allocate money • Acquire and evaluate information • Exercise leadership	• Advocate and influence • Solve problems and make decisions • Plan • Use information technology and communications

To The Teacher

PROGRAM OVERVIEW

> **Excellent English: Language Skills for Success** equips students with the grammar and skills they need to access community resources, while developing the foundation for long-term career and academic success.

Excellent English is a four-level, grammar-oriented series for English learners featuring a *Grammar Picture Dictionary* approach to vocabulary building and grammar acquisition. An accessible and predictable sequence of lessons in each unit systematically builds language and math skills around life-skill topics. *Excellent English* is tightly correlated to all of the major standards for adult instruction.

What has led the *Excellent English* team to develop this new series? The program responds to the large and growing need for a new generation of adult materials that provides a more academic alternative to existing publications. *Excellent English* is a natural response to the higher level of aspirations of today's adult learners. Stronger reading and writing skills, greater technological proficiency, and a deeper appreciation for today's global economy—increasingly, prospective employees across virtually all industries must exhibit these skill sets to be successful. Interviews with a wide range of administrators, instructors, and students underscore the need for new materials that more quickly prepare students for the vocational and academic challenges they must meet to be successful.

The Complete Excellent English Program

- The **Student Book** features twelve 16-page units that integrate listening, speaking, reading, writing, grammar, math, and pronunciation skills with life-skill topics, critical thinking activities, and civics concepts.

- The **Student Book with Audio Highlights** provides students with audio recordings of all of the Grammar Picture Dictionary, pronunciation, and conversation models in the Student Book.

- The **Workbook with Audio CD** is an essential companion to the Student Book. It provides:
  - Supplementary practice activities correlated to the Student Book.
  - Application lessons that carry vital, standards-based learning objectives through its *Family Connection*, *Community Connection*, *Career Connection*, and *Technology Connection* lessons.

- Practice tests that encourage students to assess their skills in a low-stakes environment, complete with listening tasks from the Workbook CD.

- The **Teacher's Edition with Tests** provides:
  - Step-by-step procedural notes for each Student Book activity.
  - Expansion activities for the Student Book, many of which offer creative tasks tied to the "big picture" scenes in each unit, including photocopiable worksheets.
  - Culture, Grammar, Academic, Vocabulary and Pronunciation Notes.
  - A two-page written test for each unit.
  - Audio scripts for audio program materials.
  - Answer keys for Student Book, Workbook, and Tests.

- The **Interactive multimedia program** incorporates and extends the learning goals of the Student Book by integrating language, literacy, and numeracy skill-building with multimedia practice on the computer. A flexible set of activities correlated to each unit builds vocabulary, listening, reading, writing, and test-taking skills.

- The **Color Overhead Transparencies** encourage instructors to present new vocabulary and grammar in fun and meaningful ways. This component provides a full color overhead transparency for each "big picture" scene, as well as transparencies of the grammar charts in each unit.

- The **Big Picture PowerPoint® CD-ROM** includes the "big picture" scenes for all four Student Books. Instructors can use this CD-ROM to project the scenes from a laptop through an LCD or data projector in class.

- The **Audio CDs** and **Audiocassettes** contain recordings for all listening activities in the Student Book. Listening passages for the unit tests are provided on a separate Assessment CD or Cassette.

- The **EZ Test® CD-ROM Test Generator** provides a databank of assessment items from which instructors can create customized tests within minutes. The EZ Test assessment materials are also available online at www.eztestonline.com.

Student Book Overview

Consult the *Welcome to Excellent English* guide on pages xiv-xix. This guide offers instructors and administrators a visual tour of one Student Book unit.

Excellent English is designed to maximize accessibility and flexibility. Each unit contains the following sequence of eight, two-page lessons that develop vocabulary and build language, grammar, and math skills around life-skill topics:

- Lesson 1: Grammar and Vocabulary (1)
- Lesson 2: Grammar Practice Plus
- Lesson 3: Listening and Conversation
- Lesson 4: Grammar and Vocabulary (2)
- Lesson 5: Grammar Practice Plus
- Lesson 6: Apply Your Knowledge
- Lesson 7: Reading and Writing
- Lesson 8: Career Connection and Check Your Progress

Each lesson in *Excellent English* is designed as a two-page spread. Lessons 1 and 4 introduce new grammar points and vocabulary sets that allow students to practice the grammar in controlled and meaningful ways. Lessons 2 and 5—the Grammar Practice Plus lessons—provide more opened-ended opportunities for students to use their new language productively. Lesson 3 allows students to hear a variety of listening inputs and to use their new language skills in conversation. Lesson 6 provides an opportunity for students to integrate all their language skills in a real-life application. In Lesson 7, students develop the more academic skills of reading and writing through explicit teaching of academic strategies and exposure to multiple text types and writing tasks. Each unit ends with Lesson 8, an exciting capstone that offers both Career Connection—a compelling "photo story" episode underscoring the vocational objectives of the series—and Check Your Progress—a self-evaluation task. Each lesson addresses a key adult standard, and these standards are indicated in the scope and sequence and in the footer at the bottom of the left-hand page in each lesson.

SPECIAL FEATURES IN EACH STUDENT BOOK UNIT

- **Grammar Picture Dictionary**. Lessons 1 and 4 introduce students to vocabulary and grammar through a picture dictionary approach. This context-rich approach allows students to acquire grammatical structures as they build vocabulary.

- **Grammar Charts**. Also in Lessons 1 and 4, new grammar points are presented in clear paradigms, providing easy reference for students and instructors.

- **"Grammar Professor" Notes**. Additional information related to key grammar points is provided at point of use through the "Grammar Professor" feature. A cheerful, red-haired character appears next to each of these additional grammar points, calling students' attention to learning points in an inviting and memorable way.

- **Math**. Learning basic math skills is critically important for success in school, on the job, and at home. As such, national and state standards for adult education mandate instruction in basic math skills. In each unit, a Math box is dedicated to helping students develop the functional numeracy skills they need for success with basic math.

- **Pronunciation**. This special feature has two major goals: (1) helping students hear and produce specific sounds, words, and minimal pairs of words so they become better listeners and speakers; and (2) addressing issues of stress, rhythm, and intonation so that students' spoken English becomes more comprehensible.

- *What about you?* Throughout each unit of the Student Book, students are encouraged to apply new language to their own lives through personalization activities.

- **"Big Picture" scenes**. Lesson 2 in each unit introduces a "big picture" scene. This scene serves as a springboard to a variety of activities provided in the Student Book, Teacher's Edition, Color Overhead Transparencies package and the Big Picture PowerPoint CD-ROM. In the Student Book, the "big picture" scene features key vocabulary and serves as a prompt for language activities that practice the grammar points of the unit. The scene features characters with distinct personalities for students to enjoy, respond to, and talk about.

- **Career-themed "photo story"**. Each unit ends with a compelling "photo story" episode. These four-panel scenes feature chapters in the life of an adult working to take the next step in his or her professional future. In Book 1, we follow Isabel as she identifies the next step she'd like to take in her career and works to get the education and training she needs to move ahead. The engaging photo story format provides students with role models as they pursue their own career and academic goals.

CIVICS CONCEPTS

Many institutions focus direct attention on the importance of civics instruction for English language learners. Civics instruction encourages students to become active and informed community members. The Teacher's Edition includes multiple *Community Connection* activities in each unit. These activities encourage learners to become more active and informed members of their communities.

ACADEMIC SKILL DEVELOPMENT

Many adult programs recognize the need to help students develop important academic skills that will facilitate lifelong learning. The *Excellent English* Student Book addresses this need through explicit teaching of reading and writing strategies, explicit presentation and practice of grammar, and academic notes in the Teacher's Edition. The Teacher's Edition also includes multiple *Academic Connection* activities in each unit. These activities encourage learners to become more successful in an academic environment.

CASAS, SCANS, EFF, AND OTHER STANDARDS

Instructors and administrators benchmark student progress against national and/or state standards for adult instruction. With this in mind, *Excellent English* carefully integrates instructional elements from a wide range of standards including CASAS, SCANS, EFF, TABE CLAS-E, the Florida Adult ESOL Syllabi, and the Los Angeles Unified School District Course Outlines. Unit-by-unit correlations of some of these standards appear in the Student Book scope and sequence on pages iv-ix. Other correlations appear in the Teacher's Edition. Here is a brief overview of our approach to meeting the key national and state standards:

- **CASAS**. Many U.S. states, including California, tie funding for adult education programs to student performance on the Comprehensive Adult Student Assessment System (CASAS). The CASAS (www.casas.org) competencies identify more than 30 essential skills that adults need in order to succeed in the classroom, workplace, and community. *Excellent English* comprehensively integrates all of the CASAS Life Skill Competencies throughout the four levels of the series.

- **SCANS**. Developed by the United States Department of Labor, SCANS is an acronym for the Secretary's Commission on Achieving Necessary Skills (wdr.doleta.gov/SCANS/). SCANS competencies are workplace skills that help people compete more effectively in today's global economy. A variety of SCANS competencies is threaded throughout the activities in each unit of *Excellent English*. The incorporation

of these competencies recognizes both the intrinsic importance of teaching workplace skills and the fact that many adult students are already working members of their communities.

- **EFF**. Equipped for the Future (EFF) is a set of standards for adult literacy and lifelong learning, developed by The National Institute for Literacy (www.nifl.gov). The organizing principle of EFF is that adults assume responsibilities in three major areas of life – as workers, as parents, and as citizens. These three areas of focus are called "role maps" in the EFF documentation. Each *Excellent English* unit addresses all three of the EFF role maps in the Student Book or Workbook.

- **Florida Adult ESOL Syllabi** provide the curriculum frameworks for all six levels of instruction; Foundations, Low Beginning, High Beginning, Low Intermediate, High Intermediate, and Advanced. The syllabi were developed by the State of Florida as a guide to include the following areas of adult literacy standards: workplace, communication (listen, speak, read, and write), technology, interpersonal communication, health and nutrition, government and community resources, consumer education, family and parenting, concepts of time and money, safety and security, and language development (grammar and pronunciation). *Excellent English* Level 1 incorporates into its instruction the vast majority of standards at the Low Beginning level.

- **TABE Complete Language Assessment System—English (CLAS-E)** has been developed by CTB/McGraw-Hill and provides administrators and teachers with accurate, reliable evaluations of adult students' English language skills. TABE CLAS-E measures students' reading, listening, writing, and speaking skills at all English proficiency levels and also assesses critically important grammar standards. TABE CLAS-E scores are linked to TABE 9 and 10, providing a battery of assessment tools that offer seamless transition from English language to adult basic education assessment.

- **Los Angeles Unified School District (LAUSD) Course Outlines.** LAUSD Competency-Based Education (CBE) Course Outlines were developed to guide teachers in lesson planning and to inform students about what they will be able to do after successful completion of their course. The CBE Course outlines focus on acquiring skills in listening, speaking, reading and writing in the context of everyday life. *Excellent English* addresses all four language skills in the contexts of home, community and work, appropriately targeting Beginning Low adult ESL students.

TECHNOLOGY

Technology plays an increasingly important role in our lives as students, workers, family members and citizens. Every unit in the Workbook includes a two-page lesson titled *Technology Connection* that focuses on some aspect of technology in our everyday lives.

Administrators and instructors are encouraged to incorporate interactive tasks from the *Excellent English* Multimedia Program into classroom and/or lab use as this package includes hours of meaningful technology-based practice of all key Student Book objectives.

The EZ Test® CD-ROM Test Generator—and its online version, available at www.eztestonline.com—allow instructors to easily create customized tests from a digital databank of assessment items.

NUMBER OF HOURS OF INSTRUCTION

The *Excellent English* program has been designed to accommodate the needs of adult classes with 80-180 hours of classroom instruction. Here are three recommended ways in which various components in the *Excellent English* program can be combined to meet student and instructor needs.

- **80-100 hours**. Instructors are encouraged to work through all of the Student Book materials. The Color Overhead Transparencies can be used to introduce and/or review materials in each unit. Instructors should also look to the Teacher's Edition for teaching suggestions and testing materials as necessary. *Time per unit: 8-10 hours.*

- **100-140 hours**. In addition to working through all of the Student Book materials, instructors are encouraged to incorporate the Workbook and the Interactive multimedia activities for supplementary practice. *Time per unit: 10-14 hours.*

- **140-180 hours**. Instructors and students working in an intensive instructional setting can take advantage of the wealth of expansion activities threaded through the Teacher's Edition to supplement the Student Book, Workbook, and Interactive multimedia materials. *Time per unit: 14-18 hours.*

ASSESSMENT

The *Excellent English* program offers instructors, students, and administrators the following wealth of resources for monitoring and assessing student progress and achievement:

- **Standardized testing formats**. *Excellent English* is comprehensively correlated to the CASAS competencies and all of the other major national and state standards for adult learning. Students have the opportunity to practice answering CASAS-style listening questions in Lessons 3 or 6 of each Student Book unit, and both listening and reading questions in the Unit tests in the Teacher's Edition and Practice tests in the Workbook. Students practice with the same items types and bubble-in answer sheets they encounter on CASAS and other standardized tests.

- **Achievement tests**. The *Excellent English* Teacher's Edition includes paper-and-pencil end-of-unit tests. In addition, the *EZ Test® CD-ROM Test Generator* provides a databank of assessment items from which instructors can create customized tests within minutes. The EZ Test assessment materials are also available online at www.eztestonline.com. These tests help students demonstrate how well they have learned the instructional content of the unit. Adult learners often show incremental increases in learning that are not always measured on the standardized tests. The achievement tests may demonstrate learning even in a short amount of instructional time. Twenty percent of each test includes questions that encourage students to apply more academic skills such as determining meaning from context, making inferences, and understanding main ideas. Practice with these question types will help prepare students who may want to enroll in academic classes.

- **Performance-based assessment**. *Excellent English* provides several ways to measure students' performance on productive tasks, including the *Writing* tasks in Lesson 7 of each Student Book unit. In addition, the Teacher's Edition suggests writing and speaking prompts that instructors can use for performance-based assessment.

- **Portfolio assessment**. A portfolio is a collection of student work that can be used to show progress. Examples of work that the instructor or the student may submit in the portfolio include writing samples, speaking rubrics, audiotapes, videotapes, or projects.

- **Self-assessment**. Self-assessment is an important part of the overall assessment picture, as it promotes student involvement and commitment to the learning process. When encouraged to assess themselves, students take more control of their learning and are better able to connect the instructional content with their own goals. The Student Book includes *Check Your Progress* activities at the end of each unit, which allow students to assess their knowledge of vocabulary and grammar. Students can chart their mastery of the key language lessons in the unit, and use this information to set new learning goals.

Welcome to Excellent English!

Grammar Picture Dictionary uses engaging illustrations to showcase target grammar and vocabulary.

Clear and thorough **grammar charts** make target grammar points accessible and easily comprehensible.

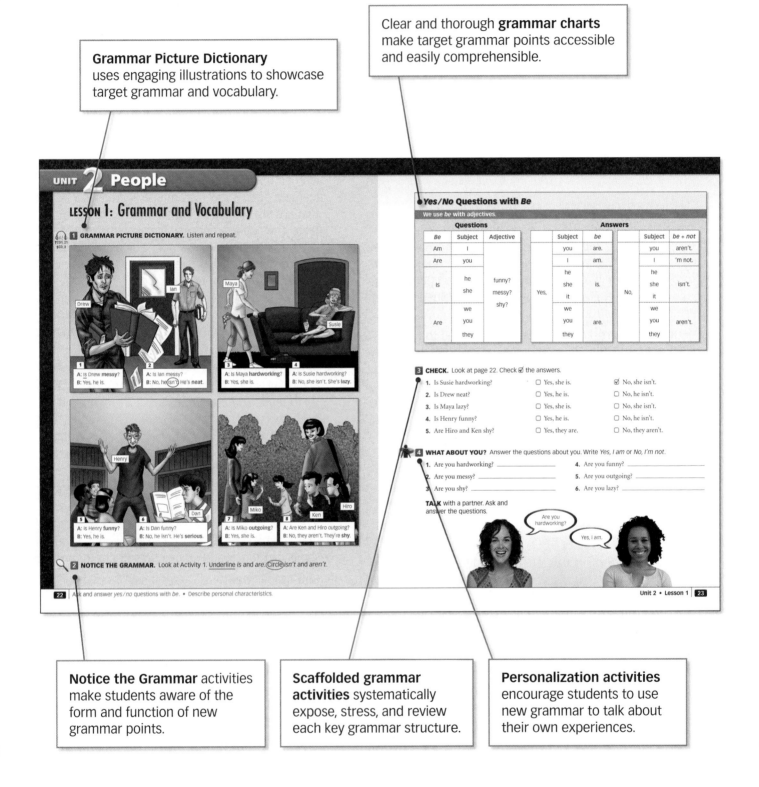

Notice the Grammar activities make students aware of the form and function of new grammar points.

Scaffolded grammar activities systematically expose, stress, and review each key grammar structure.

Personalization activities encourage students to use new grammar to talk about their own experiences.

Big Picture activities provide rich opportunities for classroom discussion and practice with new language.

LESSON 2: Grammar Practice Plus

1 WRITE. Complete the sentences. Use *is* or *are*.

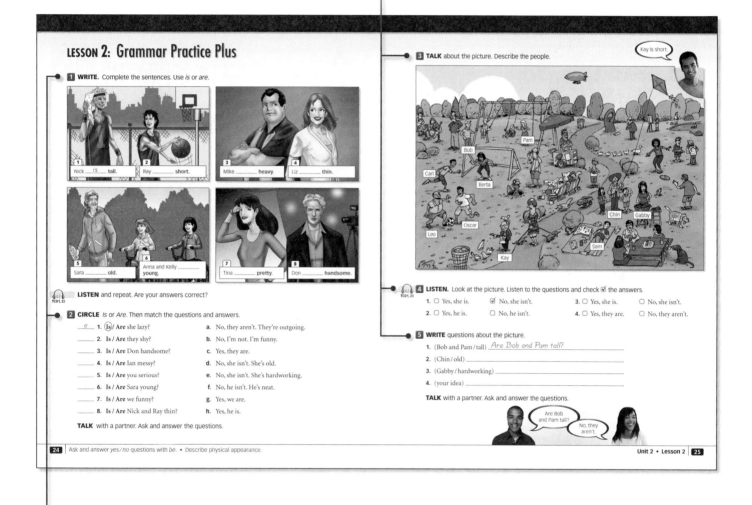

1. Nick ___is___ tall.
2. Ray _____ short.
3. Mike _____ heavy.
4. Liz _____ thin.
5. Sara _____ old.
6. Anna and Kelly _____ young.
7. Tina _____ pretty.
8. Don _____ handsome.

LISTEN and repeat. Are your answers correct?
TCD1, 22

2 CIRCLE *Is* or *Are*. Then match the questions and answers.

___e___ 1. (Is)/ Are she lazy?   a. No, they aren't. They're outgoing.

_____ 2. Is / Are they shy?   b. No, I'm not. I'm funny.

_____ 3. Is / Are Don handsome?   c. Yes, they are.

_____ 4. Is / Are Ian messy?   d. No, she isn't. She's old.

_____ 5. Is / Are you serious?   e. No, she isn't. She's hardworking.

_____ 6. Is / Are Sara young?   f. No, he isn't. He's neat.

_____ 7. Is / Are we funny?   g. Yes, we are.

_____ 8. Is / Are Nick and Ray thin?   h. Yes, he is.

TALK with a partner. Ask and answer the questions.

3 TALK about the picture. Describe the people.

Kay is short.

4 LISTEN. Look at the picture. Listen to the questions and check ☑ the answers.
TCD1, 23

1. ☐ Yes, she is.   ☑ No, she isn't.
2. ☐ Yes, he is.   ☐ No, he isn't.
3. ☐ Yes, she is.   ☐ No, she isn't.
4. ☐ Yes, they are. ☐ No, they aren't.

5 WRITE questions about the picture.

1. (Bob and Pam / tall) _Are Bob and Pam tall?_
2. (Chin / old) _____
3. (Gabby / hardworking) _____
4. (your idea) _____

TALK with a partner. Ask and answer the questions.

Are Bob and Pam tall?

No, they aren't.

24   Ask and answer yes/no questions with be. • Describe physical appearance.

Unit 2 • Lesson 2   25

Grammar Practice Plus lessons introduce additional vocabulary while recycling and practicing the target grammar.

Listening comprehension activities provide students with opportunities to build practical listening skills.

Life skills-based listening activities integrate grammar and vocabulary to provide students with models of everyday conversation.

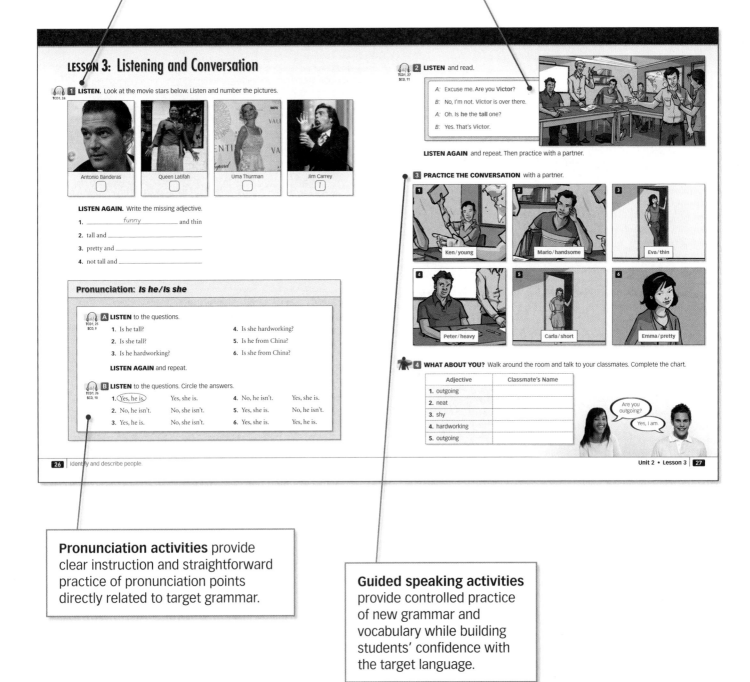

LESSON 3: Listening and Conversation

1 LISTEN. Look at the movie stars below. Listen and number the pictures.
TCD1, 24

Antonio Banderas   Queen Latifah   Uma Thurman   Jim Carrey (1)

LISTEN AGAIN. Write the missing adjective.

1. _____funny_____ and thin
2. tall and _____
3. pretty and _____
4. not tall and _____

Pronunciation: Is he/Is she

A LISTEN to the questions.
TCD1, 25
SCD, 9

1. Is he tall?
2. Is she tall?
3. Is he hardworking?
4. Is she hardworking?
5. Is he from China?
6. Is she from China?

LISTEN AGAIN and repeat.

B LISTEN to the questions. Circle the answers.
TCD1, 26
SCD, 10

1. Yes, he is.   Yes, she is.   4. No, he isn't.   Yes, she is.
2. No, he isn't.   No, she isn't.   5. Yes, she is.   No, he isn't.
3. Yes, he is.   No, she isn't.   6. Yes, she is.   Yes, he is.

26   Identify and describe people.

2 LISTEN and read.
TCD1, 27
SCD, 11

A: Excuse me. Are you **Victor**?
B: No, I'm not. Victor is over there.
A: Oh. Is **he** the **tall** one?
B: Yes. That's Victor.

LISTEN AGAIN and repeat. Then practice with a partner.

3 PRACTICE THE CONVERSATION with a partner.

1 Ken / young
2 Mario / handsome
3 Eva / thin
4 Peter / heavy
5 Carla / short
6 Emma / pretty

4 WHAT ABOUT YOU? Walk around the room and talk to your classmates. Complete the chart.

Adjective	Classmate's Name
1. outgoing	
2. neat	
3. shy	
4. hardworking	
5. outgoing	

Are you outgoing?

Yes, I am.

Unit 2 • Lesson 3   27

Pronunciation activities provide clear instruction and straightforward practice of pronunciation points directly related to target grammar.

Guided speaking activities provide controlled practice of new grammar and vocabulary while building students' confidence with the target language.

Be Careful!

Add **s** for plural nouns.
I have two teachers.

Add **'s** for possessive nouns.
This is the teacher's book.

Apply Your Knowledge lessons provide students with opportunities to practice listening, speaking, reading, and writing skills in real-world situations.

A **Grammar Professor** calls students' attention to additional grammar points in an inviting and memorable way.

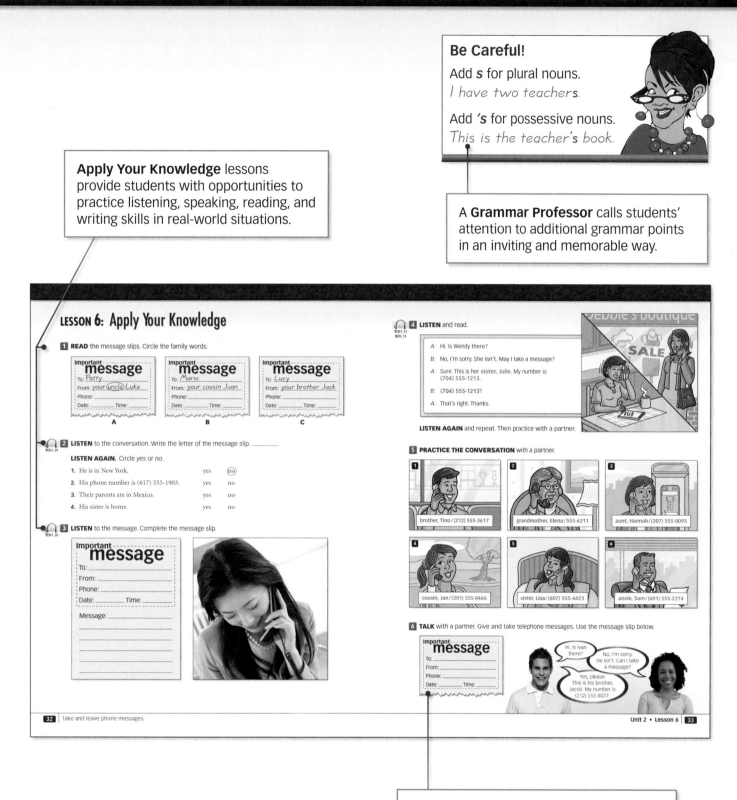

LESSON 6: Apply Your Knowledge

1 **READ** the message slips. Circle the family words.

Important
message
To: *Patty*
From: *your uncle Luke*
Phone:
Date: _____ Time: _____
A

Important
message
To: *Maria*
From: *your cousin Juan*
Phone:
Date: _____ Time: _____
B

Important
message
To: *Lucy*
From: *your brother Jack*
Phone:
Date: _____ Time: _____
C

2 **LISTEN** to the conversation. Write the letter of the message slip. _____
TCD1, 29

LISTEN AGAIN. Circle *yes* or *no.*

1. He is in New York.   yes   (no)
2. His phone number is (617) 555-1903.   yes   no
3. Their parents are in Mexico.   yes   no
4. His sister is home.   yes   no

3 **LISTEN** to the message. Complete the message slip.
TCD1, 30

Important
message
To: _____
From: _____
Phone: _____
Date: _____ Time: _____

Message: _____
_____
_____
_____
_____

4 **LISTEN** and read.
TCD1, 31
SCD, 13

A: Hi. Is Wendy there?

B: No, I'm sorry. She isn't. May I take a message?

A: Sure. This is her sister, Julie. My number is (704) 555-1213.

B: (704) 555-1213?

A: That's right. Thanks.

LISTEN AGAIN and repeat. Then practice with a partner.

5 **PRACTICE THE CONVERSATION** with a partner.

1 brother, Tino / (212) 555-3617

2 grandmother, Elena / 555-6211

3 aunt, Hannah / (207) 555-0095

4 cousin, Jan / (301) 555-0466

5 sister, Lisa / (607) 555-4423

6 uncle, Sam / (601) 555-2274

6 **TALK** with a partner. Give and take telephone messages. Use the message slip below.

Important
message
To: _____
From: _____
Phone: _____
Date: _____ Time: _____

Hi. Is Ivan there?

No, I'm sorry. He isn't. Can I take a message?

Yes, please. This is his brother, Jacob. My number is (212) 555-8077.

32 | Take and leave phone messages.

Unit 2 • Lesson 6 | **33**

Message slips, receipts, job applications, and other real-life tools prepare students to succeed in their communities.

Pre-reading tasks activate prior knowledge and introduce the reading passage.

A series of **highly-scaffolded tasks** culminates in an academic or practical writing task.

Reading and Writing Tips help students develop critical academic skills.

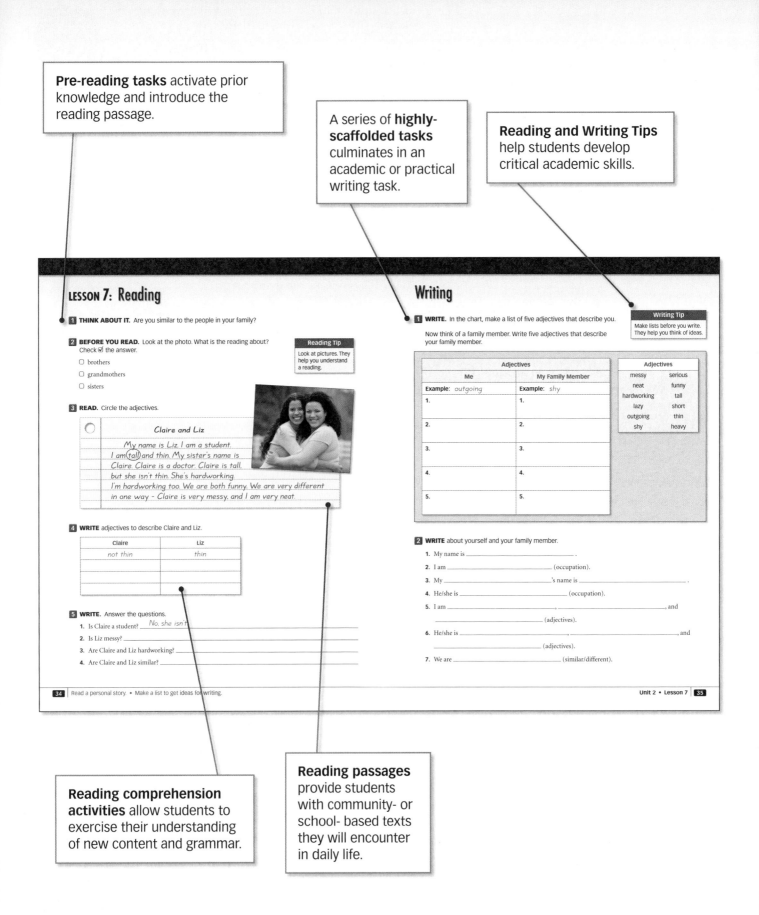

LESSON 7: Reading

1 THINK ABOUT IT. Are you similar to the people in your family?

2 BEFORE YOU READ. Look at the photo. What is the reading about? Check ☑ the answer.

> **Reading Tip**
> Look at pictures. They help you understand a reading.

- ☐ brothers
- ☐ grandmothers
- ☐ sisters

3 READ. Circle the adjectives.

> ### Claire and Liz
>
> My name is Liz. I am a student. I am (tall) and thin. My sister's name is Claire. Claire is a doctor. Claire is tall, but she isn't thin. She's hardworking. I'm hardworking too. We are both funny. We are very different in one way – Claire is very messy, and I am very neat.

4 WRITE adjectives to describe Claire and Liz.

Claire	Liz
not thin	thin

5 WRITE. Answer the questions.

1. Is Claire a student? _No, she isn't_
2. Is Liz messy? _____
3. Are Claire and Liz hardworking? _____
4. Are Claire and Liz similar? _____

Writing

1 WRITE. In the chart, make a list of five adjectives that describe you.

> **Writing Tip**
> Make lists before you write. They help you think of ideas.

Now think of a family member. Write five adjectives that describe your family member.

Adjectives		Adjectives	
Me	**My Family Member**	messy	serious
Example: outgoing	**Example:** shy	neat	funny
1.	1.	hardworking	tall
2.	2.	lazy	short
3.	3.	outgoing	thin
4.	4.	shy	heavy
5.	5.		

2 WRITE about yourself and your family member.

1. My name is _____ .
2. I am _____ (occupation).
3. My _____ 's name is _____ .
4. He/she is _____ (occupation).
5. I am _____ , _____ , and _____ (adjectives).
6. He/she is _____ , _____ , and _____ (adjectives).
7. We are _____ (similar/different).

34 Read a personal story. • Make a list to get ideas for writing.

Unit 2 • Lesson 7 35

Reading comprehension activities allow students to exercise their understanding of new content and grammar.

Reading passages provide students with community- or school- based texts they will encounter in daily life.

Career-themed photo story provides students with role models for improving their educational and/or career prospects.

Check Your Progress ensures student comprehension and retention of each unit's target grammar and vocabulary.

Career Connection

1 READ AND LISTEN. Then practice with a partner.
TCD1, 32

Panel 1: How's the new boss? / She's tall and pretty.

Panel 2: I mean, how is she as a boss? / Well, Laura is hardworking, organized, and friendly, I guess.

Panel 3: Sounds like a good boss.

Panel 4: I'm hardworking, organized and friendly, too.

2 WRITE. List adjectives for Isabel and Laura.

3 WHAT ABOUT YOU? List adjectives for you. Write a job or an occupation for each adjective.

Adjective	Job or Occupation
Example: organized	office assistant

Check Your Progress!

Skill	Circle the answer.	Is it correct?
A. Ask yes/no questions with *be*.	1. **Am / Is / Are** you hardworking?	☐
	2. **Am / Is / Are** Mike tall?	☐
	3. **Am / Is / Are** I funny?	☐

| | | | Number Correct | 0 | 1 | 2 | 3 |

Skill	Circle the answer.	Is it correct?
B. Use possessive and plural nouns.	4. Her two **sister's / sisters** are pretty.	☐
	5. His **mother's / mothers** name is Ann.	☐
	6. My **brother's / brothers** are young.	☐

| | | | Number Correct | 0 | 1 | 2 | 3 |

Skill	Circle the answer.	Is it correct?
C. Describe people.	7. She's not shy. She's **tall / outgoing**.	☐
	8. We're not messy. We're **lazy / neat**.	☐
	9. They're not tall. They're **short / heavy**.	☐

| | | | Number Correct | 0 | 1 | 2 | 3 |

Skill	Circle the answer.	Is it correct?
D. Describe family members.	10. My mother's sister is my **aunt / daughter**.	☐
	11. My mother's mother is my **sister / grandmother**.	☐
	12. My aunt's husband is my **father / uncle**.	☐

| | | | Number Correct | 0 | 1 | 2 | 3 |

COUNT the number of correct answers above. Fill in the bubbles.

Chart Your Success				
Skill	Need more practice	Okay	Good	Excellent!
A. Ask yes/no questions with *be*.	⓪	①	②	③
B. Use possessive and plural nouns.	⓪	①	②	③
C. Describe people.	⓪	①	②	③
D. Describe family members.	⓪	①	②	③

Letters and Numbers

TCD1, 2

1 **LISTEN** and repeat the letters.

Aa	Bb	Cc	Dd	Ee	Ff	Gg	Hh	Ii	Jj	Kk	Ll	Mm
Nn	Oo	Pp	Qq	Rr	Ss	Tt	Uu	Vv	Ww	Xx	Yy	Zz

LISTEN AGAIN. Point to the letters you hear.

TCD1, 3

2 **LISTEN** and repeat the numbers.

1	2	3	4	5	6	7	8	9	10	11	12	13	14
15	16	17	18	19	20	30	40	50	60	70	80	90	100

LISTEN AGAIN. Point to the numbers you hear.

TCD1, 4

3 **LISTEN** and read.

> A: Hi, my name is Ann.
>
> B: Hi, Ann. My name is Sandra.
>
> A: How do you spell your name?
>
> B: S-a-n-d-r-a.

LISTEN AGAIN and repeat.

4 **TALK** to four classmates. Write their names.

1. _____

2. _____

3. _____

4. _____

Hi, my name is Luis.

How do you spell your name?

Classroom Directions

5 **GRAMMAR PICTURE DICTIONARY.** Listen and read.

1. Write your name.
2. Open your book.
3. Turn to page 15.
4. Take out a pen.
5. Stand up.
6. Sit down.
7. Raise your hand.
8. Listen.
9. Read.

LISTEN AGAIN and repeat.

6 **TALK.** Read the sentences to a partner. Your partner does the actions.

Grammar: Parts of Speech

1 **LISTEN** and repeat.

NOUNS

A noun is a person, a place, or a thing.

| 1 a teacher | 2 a school | 3 a book |

VERBS

A verb is an action word.

| 4 study | 5 talk | 6 read |

ADJECTIVES

An adjective describes a noun.

| 7 red | 8 happy | 9 tall |

PRONOUNS

Singular Pronouns (1)	
I	
You	
He	
She	
It	

Plural Pronouns (2 or 2+)	
We	
You	
They	

 2 **LISTEN** and repeat the sentences.

TCD1, 7

Sentences

Subject (Noun or Pronoun)	Verb	Noun/Adjective
I	study	English.
You	read	books.
He She The teacher It	is	tall.
We You They Ann and Sandra	walk	to school.

TALK. Read the sentences to a partner.

LESSON 1: Grammar and Vocabulary

1 GRAMMAR PICTURE DICTIONARY. Listen and repeat.

TCD1, 8
SCD, 2

1 My **first name** is Diana.
My **last name** is Montego.

2 My **address** is 351 East 4th Street, Washington, D.C.

3 My **zip code** is 20021.

4 My **telephone number** is (202) 555-4376.

5 My **email address** is dmontego27@college.edu.

6 I am **single**.

7 We are **students**.

8 Mr. and Mrs. Green are my **teachers**.

9 They are **married**.

2 NOTICE THE GRAMMAR. Look at Activity 1. Circle *am, is,* and *are*.

Affirmative Statements With *Be*

We use contractions (*I'm*) more than long forms (*I am*).

We use the verb *to be* (am, is, are) with personal information.

Subject	*be*		Contractions
I	am	married.	I am = I'm
You	are	single.	You are = You're
He			He is = He's
She	is	from China.	She is = She's
It			It is = It's
We		students.	We are = We're
You	are	married.	You are = You're
They		from India.	They are = They're

---

3 **WRITE.** Complete the sentences. Use *am, is,* or *are*.

1. My name ___is___ Sam Ali.

2. I _____ from Egypt.

3. My address _____ 5020 Trade St.

4. My email address _____ samali@heyyou.net.

5. I _____ single.

6. My teachers _____ Mr. and Mrs. Smith.

7. They _____ married.

Name: _____Ali_____Sam_____
           Last   First

Address: ___5020 Trade St,_____
        #   Street

City: ___Chicago___ Zip code: __75212__

married   (single)

---

4 **WHAT ABOUT YOU?** Complete the sentences about you.

1. My first name is _____.

2. My last name is _____.

3. I'm from _____.

TALK. Read your sentences to a partner.

My first name is Mariya. My last name is Petrov. I'm from Russia.

LESSON 2: Grammar Practice Plus

Negative Statements With *Be*

Subject	*be*	*not*		Contractions
I	am		a student.	I am not = I'm not
You	are		a teacher.	You are not = You're not/you aren't
He				He is not = He's not/He isn't
She	is	not	from China.	She is not = She's not/She isn't
It				It is not = It's not/It isn't
We			from Mexico.	We are not = We're not/We aren't
You	are		married.	You are not = You're not/You aren't
They			students.	They are not = They're not/They aren't

1 **WRITE.** Complete the sentences. Use *am not*, *is not*, or *are not*.

1. She is from Somalia. She _____*is not*_____ from China.

2. We are married. We _____ single.

3. My address is 23 Main Street. It _____ 32 Main Street.

4. They are teachers. They _____ students.

5. You are from China. You _____ from Mexico.

6. I am single. I _____ married.

7. He is from Mexico. He _____ from Cuba.

8. Jack and Mary are students. They _____ teachers.

2 **WHAT ABOUT YOU?** Complete the chart. Use the words in the box.

I'm _____.	I'm not _____.
Example: *single*	Example: *married*

single	from Mexico
married	from China
a teacher	_____
a student	_____

TALK. Read your sentences to a partner.

| Make statements with *be*. • Tell where people are from.

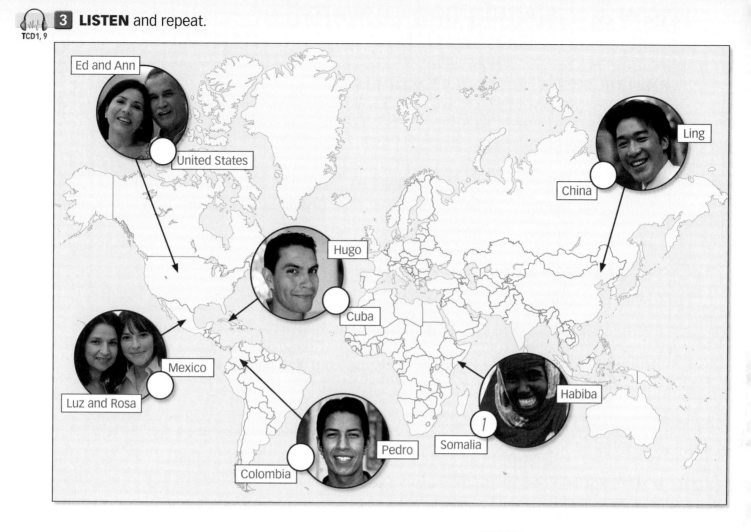

3 LISTEN and repeat.

TCD1, 9

4 LISTEN AGAIN. Number the countries.

5 TALK. Look at the picture.
What countries are the people from?

Habiba is from Somalia.

Luz is from Mexico.

6 WRITE. Complete the sentences. Use *is, isn't, are,* or *aren't.*

1. Habiba _____is_____ from Somalia.

2. Ed and Ann _____ from Colombia.

3. Luz and Rosa _____ from Mexico.

4. Ling _____ from China.

5. Hugo _____ from the United States.

LESSON 3: Listening and Conversation

Pronunciation: Stress in Numbers

A LISTEN and repeat.

TCD1, 10
SCD, 3

1. thirteen   thirty   4. sixteen   sixty
2. fourteen   forty   5. seventeen   seventy
3. fifteen   fifty   6. eighteen   eighty

B LISTEN and circle the word you hear.

TCD1, 11
SCD, 4

1. (13)   30   3. 15   50   5. 17   70
2. 19   90   4. 116   160   6. 1410   4010

C TALK. Work with a partner. Circle the word your partner says.

1. 14   40   2. 16   60   3. 18   80

1 LISTEN and circle the correct letter.

TCD1, 12

1. **A.** 5040 Broad Street   **B.** 1514 Broad Street   **C.** 1540 Broad Street
2. **A.** (305) 555-1723   **B.** (305) 555-7023   **C.** (305) 555-0723
3. **A.** 6013 Market Street   **B.** 1630 Market Street   **C.** 6030 Market Street

2 LISTEN. Where are the people from? Write the country. Use the words in the box.

TCD1, 13

| China | Cuba | Korea | Colombia | Mexico |

1 Mary: _____

2 Roberto: _____

3 Han: _____

Introduce yourself. • Understand and pronounce numbers.

3 **LISTEN** and read.

TCD1, 14
SCD, 5

> A: Hi, my name's **Manuel**. I'm from **Brazil**.
>
> B: Hi, **Manuel**. My name's **Sue**. I'm from **Canada**. It's nice to meet you.
>
> A: Nice to meet you, too.

LISTEN AGAIN and repeat. Then practice with a partner.

4 **WHAT ABOUT YOU?** Talk to six classmates. Use the conversation in Activity 3. Complete the chart.

Classmate's name	Country (or City)
Example: *Ricardo*	**Example:** *Cuba*

5 **GAME.** Work in a small group. Play the game.

LESSON 4: Grammar and Vocabulary

1 GRAMMAR PICTURE DICTIONARY. Listen and repeat.

TCD1, 15
SCD, 6

1 She is **a doctor**.

2 He is **a police officer**.

3 He is **a dentist**.

4 He is **an office assistant**.

5 She is **a housekeeper**.

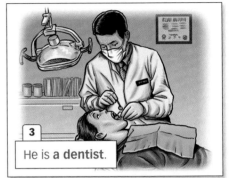

6 They are **taxi drivers**.

7 They are **servers**.

8 He is **a cook**.

9 He is **an actor**.

10 She is **a salesclerk**.

11 They are **construction workers**.

12 He is **a nurse**.

2 NOTICE THE GRAMMAR. Look at Activity 1. Underline *a* and *an*. Circle the words that end in *s*.

12 | Talk about occupations. • Use singular and plural nouns.

Singular and Plural Nouns

Singular (1)
Use *a* before singular nouns that start with a consonant (b, c, d, f, g, h, j, k, l, m, n, p, q, r, s, t, v, w, x, y, z)
Use *an* before singular nouns that start with a vowel (a, e, i, o, and u).

	Article	Singular Noun
I am He is You are	a	waiter. └── consonants firefighter.
	an	┌── vowel office assistant.

Plural (2+)
Add *s* to most nouns to make the nouns plural.

	Plural Noun
They are	waiters.
We are	firefighters.
You are	office assistants.

---

3 WRITE. Complete the sentences. Use *a* or *an*.

1. I am ____*a*____ server.

2. Lydia is _____ actress.

3. Seth is _____ taxi driver.

4. She is _____ construction worker.

5. Tom is _____ office assistant.

4 CIRCLE the correct words.

1. I am **a teacher** / **teachers**.

2. Tina and Miko are **a cook** / **cooks**.

3. You and Mira are **a housekeeper** / **housekeepers**.

4. She is **a doctor** / **doctors**.

5. Hugo and I are **a police officer** / **police officers**.

6. Sam is **a salesclerk** / **salesclerks**.

5 WHAT ABOUT YOU? Talk to a partner about *your* occupation.

What's your occupation?

I'm a student. What about you?

I'm a salesclerk.

LESSON 5: Grammar Practice Plus

These plural nouns are irregular.

1 LISTEN and repeat.

TCD1, 16

man	men
woman	women
child	children
person	people

2 WHAT ABOUT YOU? Write the number.

1. _____ men are in my class.

2. _____ children are in my class.

3. _____ women are in my class.

4. _____ people are in my class.

3 WRITE. Complete the sentences about people in Diana's English class.

	👨	👩
🏗️	2	1
👩‍⚕️	1	3
👨‍🍳	3	0
👮	0	2

1. Two _____*men*_____ are construction workers.

2. One _____ is a construction worker.

3. Three _____ are nurses.

4. Three men are _____.

5. Two women are _____.

6. Four _____ are nurses.

4 **TALK** about the picture.

5 **LISTEN** and write the country. Then look at the picture and complete the chart.

TCD1, 17

Name	Country	Man or woman?	Job
Musa	*Somalia*	*man*	*nurse*
Luis			
Lily			
Ivan			

6 **WRITE.** Write sentences about the people in the chart in Activity 5.

Example: *Musa is a man. He's a nurse. He's from Somalia.*

_____

_____

_____

TALK. Read your sentences to a partner.

LESSON 6: Apply Your Knowledge

1 LISTEN. Complete the sentences.

1. My name _is Anna Park_____.

2. My telephone number _____.

3. My address _____.

4. My zip code _____.

5. I'm _____ and _____.

2 WRITE. Complete the form.

School Registration Form

Name: ___Anna_____ ___Park_____
             First   Last

Address: _____ _Pine Street_____
                            Street

City: __Washington___ State: _D.C.__ Zip: _____

Telephone number: (_____) _555__-_____

Marital status: ☐ Married   Gender: ☐ Male
             ☐ Single   ☑ Female

Occupation: _____

Gender

Male   **Female**

Math: Recognize Patterns

SOCIAL SECURITY
000-10-9999
THIS NUMBER HAS BEEN ESTABLISHED FOR
Ramon Suarez
Ramon Suarez
SIGNATURE

Social Security Number

SUNNY GROVE HOSPITAL
Employee's Name: _Evan Jones_
Employee's ID: (S552)
Expires: 2/5/2012

Employee Badge Number

MATCH the number to the type of information.

_b_ 1. Social Security number   **a.** 9321 South Street

___ 2. telephone number   **b.** 042-43-2246

___ 3. badge number for work   **c.** (305) 555-3322

___ 4. address   **d.** 22101

___ 5. zip code   **e.** A287

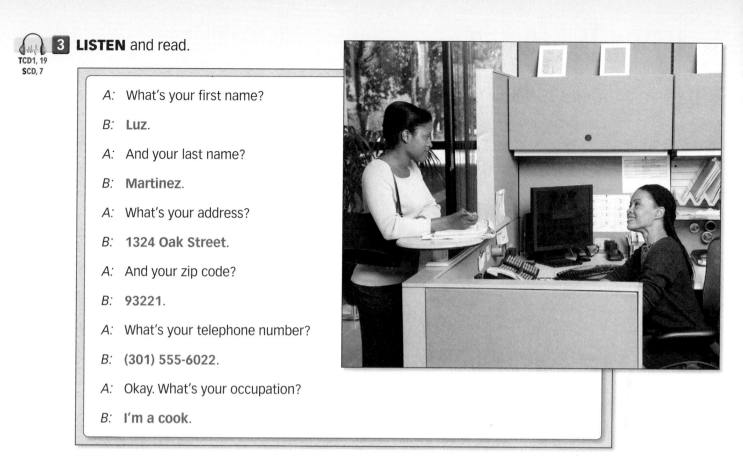

3 LISTEN and read.

TCD1, 19
SCD, 7

A: What's your first name?

B: **Luz**.

A: And your last name?

B: **Martinez**.

A: What's your address?

B: **1324 Oak Street**.

A: And your zip code?

B: **93221**.

A: What's your telephone number?

B: **(301) 555-6022**.

A: Okay. What's your occupation?

B: **I'm a cook**.

LISTEN AGAIN and repeat. Then practice with a partner.

4 PRACTICE THE CONVERSATION with a partner. Ask and answer questions. Use the forms below.

Name: _____Mark_____ _____Cooper_____
           First   Last

Address: _____302 6th Street_____
           Street

City: _Chicago_ State: _IL_ Zip: _60620_

Telephone number: (_312_) _555_ – _6811_

Marital status: ☐ Married   Gender: ☑ Male
           ☑ Single   ☐ Female

Occupation: _____police officer_____

Name: _____Wen_____ _____Chin_____
           First   Last

Address: _____27 Center Street_____
           Street

City: _Sacramento_ State: _CA_ Zip: _93114_

Telephone number: (_916_) _555_ – _8095_

Marital status: ☑ Married   Gender: ☐ Male
           ☐ Single   ☑ Female

Occupation: _____dentist_____

What's your first name?

Mark.

LESSON 7: Reading

1 **THINK ABOUT IT.** What is a capital letter? When do we write a capital letter?

2 **BEFORE YOU READ.** Look at the letter below. Circle the names of people.

Reading Tip

Look for capital letters. They help you find names.

3 **READ** the letter. Underline the names of countries and cities.

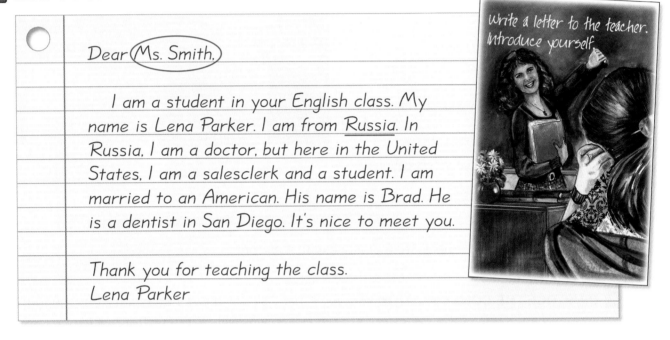

Dear (Ms. Smith,)

   I am a student in your English class. My name is Lena Parker. I am from Russia. In Russia, I am a doctor, but here in the United States, I am a salesclerk and a student. I am married to an American. His name is Brad. He is a dentist in San Diego. It's nice to meet you.

Thank you for teaching the class.
Lena Parker

Write a letter to the teacher. Introduce yourself.

4 **CIRCLE** *yes* or *no*.

1. Ms. Smith is a teacher.   (yes)   no
2. The letter is to Ms. Parker.   yes   no
3. The student is Brad Parker.   yes   no
4. Lena is from Russia.   yes   no
5. Lena is single.   yes   no

5 **WRITE.** Look at the letter in Activity 3. Find the words with a capital letter. Write them below.

_____Dear_____   _____   _____

_____   _____   _____

_____   _____   _____

_____   _____   _____

Writing

1 **WRITE** the sentences again. Use capital letters.

Example: my name is hector ruiz.

My name is Hector Ruiz.

1. my name is vera king.

   _____

2. i am from china.

   _____

3. we are from miami, florida.

   _____

4. he is in mr. green's class.

   _____

5. dr. johnson is from canada.

   _____

<table>
<tr><td>Writing Tip</td></tr>
</table>

Writing Tip

Use a capital letter with:

- first and last names (Lena Parker)
- streets (3572 Trade Street)
- cities (San Diego)
- states (California)
- the first letter of each sentence (My name is Lena Parker.)
- I (I am from Russia.)
- Mr., Mrs., Ms., Dr. (This is Dr. Smith.)

Title	Use for	Pronunciation
Mr.	single and married men	*mister*
Mrs.	married women	*missiz*
Ms.	single and married women	*miz*
Dr.	doctors	*doctor*

2 **WRITE** your name and address on the envelope.

From:

Name ⟶ Lena Parker

Street address ⟶ 3572 Trade St.

City, state, zip code ⟶ San Diego, CA 92101

USA

_____ (name)

_____ (address)

_____ (city, state, zip)

1 READ and listen. Then practice with a partner.

Good morning. I'm Laura Markham. I'm the new hospital administrator.

Welcome. I'm Isabel Thompson, your office assistant.

1

Please complete this form. And may I have your passport and social security card?

2

Sure. Here they are.

Thanks. I'll make copies.

3

Here is your hospital ID.

Thank you.

4

2 CHECK ☑ yes or no.

1.	Laura Markham is an office assistant.	☐ yes	☑ no
2.	Isabel Thompson is an office assistant.	☐ yes	☐ no
3.	Isabel and Laura work in a school.	☐ yes	☐ no
4.	Laura has a social security card.	☐ yes	☐ no
5.	Laura is the new boss.	☐ yes	☐ no

Check Your Progress!

Skill	Circle the answer.	Is it correct?			
A. Use *be* with personal information.	1. My name **am** / **is** / **are** Lena. 2. I **am** / **is** / **are** a student. 3. We **am** / **is** / **are** from Cuba.	☐ ☐ ☐			
	Number Correct	0	1	2	3
B. Use singular and plural nouns.	4. He is **a doctor** / **doctors**. 5. We are **a teacher** / **teachers**. 6. They are **a nurse** / **nurses**.	☐ ☐ ☐			
	Number Correct	0	1	2	3
C. Give personal information.	7. My **zip code** / **phone number** is (703) 555-9055. 8. The **address** / **email address** is 35 South Street. 9. He isn't married. He's **female** / **single**.	☐ ☐ ☐			
	Number Correct	0	1	2	3
D. Say occupations.	10. She is **a police officer** / **a nurse**. 11. Jim is **a cook** / **a construction worker**. 12. I am **a dentist** / **a housekeeper**.	☐ ☐ ☐			
	Number Correct	0	1	2	3

COUNT the number of correct answers above. Fill in the bubbles.

Chart Your Success				
Skill	Need more practice	Okay	Good	Excellent!
A. Use *be* with personal information.	⓪	①	②	③
B. Use singular and plural nouns.	⓪	①	②	③
C. Give personal information.	⓪	①	②	③
D. Say occupations.	⓪	①	②	③

LESSON 1: Grammar and Vocabulary

1 **GRAMMAR PICTURE DICTIONARY.** Listen and repeat.

TCD1, 21
SCD, 8

1
A: Is Drew **messy**?
B: Yes, he is.

2
A: Is Ian messy?
B: No, he isn't. He's **neat**.

3
A: Is Maya **hardworking**?
B: Yes, she is.

4
A: Is Susie hardworking?
B: No, she isn't. She's **lazy**.

5
A: Is Henry **funny**?
B: Yes, he is.

6
A: Is Dan funny?
B: No, he isn't. He's **serious**.

7
A: Is Miko **outgoing**?
B: Yes, she is.

8
A: Are Ken and Hiro outgoing?
B: No, they aren't. They're **shy**.

2 **NOTICE THE GRAMMAR.** Look at Activity 1. Underline *is* and *are*. Circle *isn't* and *aren't*.

Yes/No Questions with Be

We use *be* with adjectives.

Questions

Be	Subject	Adjective
Am	I	
Are	you	
Is	he she	funny? messy? shy?
Are	we you they	

Answers

	Subject	*be*
Yes,	you	are.
	I	am.
	he she it	is.
	we you they	are.

	Subject	*be + not*
No,	you	aren't.
	I	'm not.
	he she it	isn't.
	we you they	aren't.

3 **CHECK.** Look at page 22. Check ☑ the answers.

1. Is Susie hardworking? ☐ Yes, she is. ☑ No, she isn't.
2. Is Drew neat? ☐ Yes, he is. ☐ No, he isn't.
3. Is Maya lazy? ☐ Yes, she is. ☐ No, she isn't.
4. Is Henry funny? ☐ Yes, he is. ☐ No, he isn't.
5. Are Hiro and Ken shy? ☐ Yes, they are. ☐ No, they aren't.

4 **WHAT ABOUT YOU?** Answer the questions about you. Write *Yes, I am* or *No, I'm not*.

1. Are you hardworking? _____ 4. Are you funny? _____
2. Are you messy? _____ 5. Are you outgoing? _____
3. Are you shy? _____ 6. Are you lazy? _____

TALK with a partner. Ask and answer the questions.

Are you hardworking?

Yes, I am.

LESSON 2: Grammar Practice Plus

1 WRITE. Complete the sentences. Use *is* or *are*.

1. Nick __is__ tall.
2. Ray ______ **short.**

3. Mike ______ **heavy.**
4. Liz ______ **thin.**

5. Sara ______ **old.**
6. Anna and Kelly ______ **young.**

7. Tina ______ **pretty.**
8. Don ______ **handsome.**

TCD1, 22

LISTEN and repeat. Are your answers correct?

2 CIRCLE *Is* or *Are*. Then match the questions and answers.

__e__ 1. (**Is**) / **Are** she lazy?	a. No, they aren't. They're outgoing.
_____ 2. **Is / Are** they shy?	b. No, I'm not. I'm funny.
_____ 3. **Is / Are** Don handsome?	c. Yes, they are.
_____ 4. **Is / Are** Ian messy?	d. No, she isn't. She's old.
_____ 5. **Is / Are** you serious?	e. No, she isn't. She's hardworking.
_____ 6. **Is / Are** Sara young?	f. No, he isn't. He's neat.
_____ 7. **Is / Are** we funny?	g. Yes, we are.
_____ 8. **Is / Are** Nick and Ray thin?	h. Yes, he is.

TALK with a partner. Ask and answer the questions.

3 **TALK** about the picture. Describe the people.

Kay is short.

4 **LISTEN.** Look at the picture. Listen to the questions and check ☑ the answers.

TCD1, 23

1. ☐ Yes, she is.   ☑ No, she isn't.   3. ☐ Yes, she is.   ☐ No, she isn't.

2. ☐ Yes, he is.   ☐ No, he isn't.   4. ☐ Yes, they are.   ☐ No, they aren't.

5 **WRITE** questions about the picture.

1. (Bob and Pam / tall) _Are Bob and Pam tall?_

2. (Chin / old) _____

3. (Gabby / hardworking) _____

4. (your idea) _____

TALK with a partner. Ask and answer the questions.

Are Bob and Pam tall?

No, they aren't.

LESSON 3: Listening and Conversation

1 **LISTEN.** Look at the movie stars below. Listen and number the pictures.

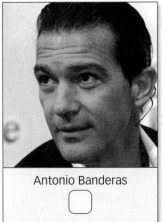

Antonio Banderas

◯

Queen Latifah

◯

Uma Thurman

◯

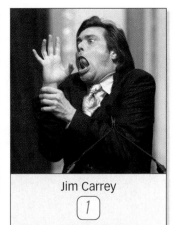

Jim Carrey

1

LISTEN AGAIN. Write the missing adjective.

1. _____ *funny* _____ and thin

2. tall and _____

3. pretty and _____

4. not tall and _____

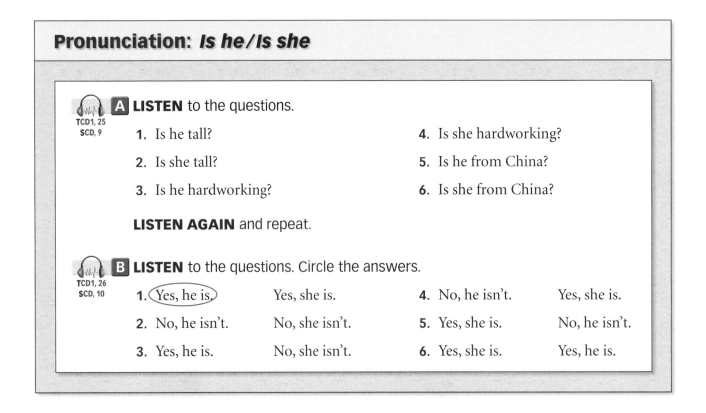

Pronunciation: *Is he / Is she*

A **LISTEN** to the questions.

1. Is he tall?

2. Is she tall?

3. Is he hardworking?

4. Is she hardworking?

5. Is he from China?

6. Is she from China?

LISTEN AGAIN and repeat.

B **LISTEN** to the questions. Circle the answers.

1. (Yes, he is.)   Yes, she is.   4. No, he isn't.   Yes, she is.

2. No, he isn't.   No, she isn't.   5. Yes, she is.   No, he isn't.

3. Yes, he is.   No, she isn't.   6. Yes, she is.   Yes, he is.

2 **LISTEN** and read.

TCD1, 27
SCD, 11

> A: Excuse me. Are you **Victor**?
>
> B: No, I'm not. **Victor** is over there.
>
> A: Oh. Is **he** the **tall** one?
>
> B: Yes. That's **Victor**.

LISTEN AGAIN and repeat. Then practice with a partner.

3 **PRACTICE THE CONVERSATION** with a partner.

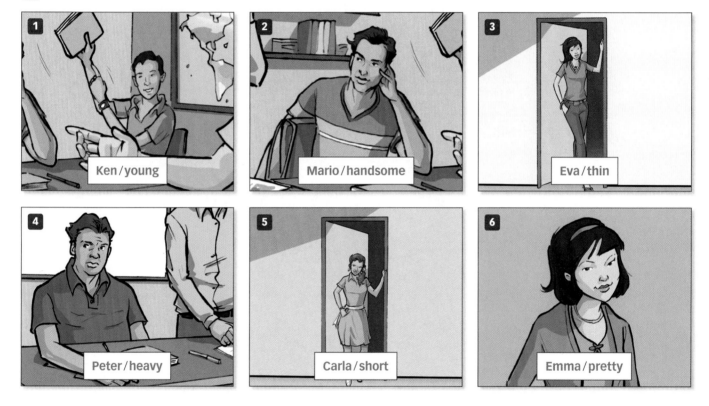

1. Ken / young
2. Mario / handsome
3. Eva / thin
4. Peter / heavy
5. Carla / short
6. Emma / pretty

4 **WHAT ABOUT YOU?** Walk around the room and talk to your classmates. Complete the chart.

Adjective	Classmate's Name
1. outgoing	
2. neat	
3. shy	
4. hardworking	
5. outgoing	

Are you outgoing?

Yes, I am.

LESSON 4: Grammar and Vocabulary

TCD1, 28
SCD, 12

1 GRAMMAR PICTURE DICTIONARY. Listen and repeat.

	Ann Wyatt's Family
	Ann Wyatt is a doctor in San Jose, California. Roger is (her) husband.
	John is Ann's **father**. Nancy is her **mother**. Nancy is John's wife.
	Roger and Ann's **daughter** is Grace, and their **son** is Paul.
	Paul and Grace's **grandfather** is John, and their **grandmother** is Nancy.
	Adam is Roger's **brother**. Mira is Adam's **wife**.
	Karen and Jenny are Ann's **sisters**.
	Karen, Jenny and Mira are Grace and Paul's **aunts**. Adam and Greg are their **uncles**.
	Dina and Cole are their **cousins**.

2 NOTICE THE GRAMMAR. Look at Activity 1. Circle *her* and *their*.

Identify family members. • Use possessive adjectives.

Possessive Adjectives

Subject	Possessive Adjective	Examples
I	my	**My** name is Mara Lane.
you	your	This is **your** teacher.
he	his	**His** sister is pretty.
she	her	**Her** daughters are Linda and Pam.
we	our	Henry is **our** son.
you	your	**Your** brother is handsome.
they	their	**Their** mother is hardworking.

3 **WRITE.** Complete the sentences. Use *my, your, his, her, our, your,* or *their*.

1. Ann has a sister. _____*Her*_____ name is Kate.

2. Ann and Roger have one daughter. _____ name is Grace.

3. They have one son. _____ name is Paul.

4. Adam has two cousins. _____ names are Ben and Finn.

5. I have one aunt. _____ name is Jenny.

6. They have three children. _____ children are shy.

7. We have two sons. _____ sons are handsome.

8. I have one uncle. _____ uncle is outgoing.

4 **WHAT ABOUT YOU?** Write about your family.

Example: I have ____*three sisters*____. ___*Their names are Luisa, Elena, and Rita*___.

1. I have _____. _____.

2. I have _____. _____.

3. I have _____. _____.

TALK. Read your sentences to a partner.

LESSON 5: Grammar Practice Plus

Possessives of Nouns

Add 's to make a noun possessive.

Ann	Ann's	I am Ann's brother.
the teacher	the teacher's	Mrs. Green is the teacher's wife.

1 **WRITE.** Look at the picture. Complete the sentences. Use possessives of nouns.

1. Helen is _____Ted's_____ mother.

2. Steven is _____ son.

3. Kristin is _____ sister.

4. Frank is _____ husband.

5. Ella is _____ wife.

6. Frank is _____ grandfather.

2 **WRITE.** Complete the sentences.

1. My _____sisters_____ (sisters / sister's) are tall.

2. Their _____ (brothers / brother's) name is John.

3. Write your _____ (mothers / mother's) address on the line.

4. His _____ (grandmothers / grandmother's) are in Florida.

5. Dara and Mia are _____ (sisters / sister's).

6. Her _____ (children / children's) are Oscar and Rosa.

Be Careful!

Add **s** for plural nouns.
I have two teachers.

Add **'s** for possessive nouns.
This is the teacher's book.

Use possessives of nouns and adjectives. • Interpret a chart.

3 **WHAT ABOUT YOU?** Write about your family in the chart.

Family Member	Name	Adjective
Father	Alberto	tall

My father's name is Alberto. He's tall.

My sister's name is Lily. She's serious.

TALK with a partner about your family.

Math: Height Charts Read the information. Answer the questions.

In most countries people measure height in centimeters.
In the United States, people measure height in feet and inches.

WOMEN	Feet and Inches	Centimeters	MEN
	6 ft. 2 in.	187.96	
	6 ft. 1 in.	185.42	Tall
	6 ft. 0 in.	182.88	
Tall	5 ft. 11 in.	180.34	
	5 ft. 10 in.	177.80	
	5 ft. 9 in.	175.26	Average height
	5 ft. 8 in.	172.72	
	5 ft. 7 in.	170.18	
	5 ft. 6 in.	167.64	
Average height	5 ft. 5 in.	165.10	
	5 ft. 4 in.	162.56	
	5 ft. 3 in.	160.02	Short
	5 ft. 2 in.	157.48	
Short	5 ft. 1 in.	154.94	
	5 ft. 0 in.	152.40	

Abbreviations
foot/feet = ft.
inch = in.
centimeter = cm

Conversions
1 inch = 2.54 cm
1 cm = .4 inch

I am 5 feet 3 inches tall.

1. Susan's height is 180 cm. She is __5__ feet __11__ inches tall. Is she short, average height, or tall? _____

2. Henri's height is 165 cm. He is _____ feet _____ inches tall. Is he short, average height, or tall? _____

3. What is your height in feet and inches? _____

LESSON 6: Apply Your Knowledge

1 **READ** the message slips. Circle the family words.

Important
message
To: _Patty_
From: _your (uncle) Luke_
Phone: _____
Date: _____ Time: _____

A

Important
message
To: _Maria_
From: _your cousin Juan_
Phone: _____
Date: _____ Time: _____

B

Important
message
To: _Lucy_
From: _your brother Jack_
Phone: _____
Date: _____ Time: _____

C

TCD1, 29

2 **LISTEN** to the conversation. Write the letter of the message slip. _____

LISTEN AGAIN. Circle *yes* or *no*.

1. He is in New York.   yes   (no)

2. His phone number is (617) 555-1903.   yes   no

3. Their parents are in Mexico.   yes   no

4. His sister is home.   yes   no

TCD1, 30

3 **LISTEN** to the message. Complete the message slip.

Important
message
To: _____
From: _____
Phone: _____
Date: _____ Time: _____

Message: _____
_____
_____
_____
_____

4 **LISTEN** and read.

TCD1, 31
SCD, 13

> A: Hi. Is Wendy there?
>
> B: No, I'm sorry. She isn't. May I take a message?
>
> A: Sure. This is her **sister, Julie.** My number is **(704) 555-1213.**
>
> B: **(704) 555-1213?**
>
> A: That's right. Thanks.

LISTEN AGAIN and repeat. Then practice with a partner.

5 **PRACTICE THE CONVERSATION** with a partner.

1	2	3
brother, Tino / (212) 555-3617	grandmother, Elena / 555-6211	aunt, Hannah / (207) 555-0095

4	5	6
cousin, Jan / (301) 555-0466	sister, Lisa / (607) 555-4423	uncle, Sam / (601) 555-2274

6 **TALK** with a partner. Give and take telephone messages. Use the message slip below.

Important
message

To: _____
From: _____
Phone: _____
Date: _____ Time: _____

Hi. Is Ivan there?

No, I'm sorry. He isn't. Can I take a message?

Yes, please. This is his brother, Jacob. My number is (212) 555-8077.

LESSON 7: Reading

1 **THINK ABOUT IT.** Are you similar to the people in your family?

2 **BEFORE YOU READ.** Look at the photo. What is the reading about? Check ☑ the answer.

- ☐ brothers
- ☐ grandmothers
- ☐ sisters

3 **READ.** Circle the adjectives.

Claire and Liz

My name is Liz. I am a student.
I am (tall) and thin. My sister's name is
Claire. Claire is a doctor. Claire is tall,
but she isn't thin. She's hardworking.
I'm hardworking too. We are both funny. We are very different
in one way – Claire is very messy, and I am very neat.

4 **WRITE** adjectives to describe Claire and Liz.

Claire	Liz
not thin	thin

5 **WRITE.** Answer the questions.

1. Is Claire a student? _No, she isn't._____

2. Is Liz messy? _____

3. Are Claire and Liz hardworking? _____

4. Are Claire and Liz similar? _____

Read a personal story. • Make a list to get ideas for writing.

Writing

1 WRITE. In the chart, make a list of five adjectives that describe you.

Now think of a family member. Write five adjectives that describe your family member.

Adjectives		Adjectives	
Me	**My Family Member**	messy	serious
Example: *outgoing*	Example: *shy*	neat	funny
1.	**1.**	hardworking	tall
		lazy	short
2.	**2.**	outgoing	thin
		shy	heavy
3.	**3.**		
4.	**4.**		
5.	**5.**		

2 WRITE about yourself and your family member.

1. My name is _____ .

2. I am _____ (occupation).

3. My _____'s name is _____ .

4. He/she is _____ (occupation).

5. I am _____, _____, and
_____ (adjectives).

6. He/she is _____, _____, and
_____ (adjectives).

7. We are _____ (similar/different).

Career Connection

1 READ AND LISTEN. Then practice with a partner.

2 WRITE. List adjectives for Isabel and Laura.

3 WHAT ABOUT YOU? List adjectives for you. Write a job or an occupation for each adjective.

	Adjective	Job or Occupation
Example:	*organized*	*office assistant*

Check Your Progress!

Skill	Circle the answer.	Is it correct?
A. Ask yes/no questions with *be*.	1. **Am / Is / Are** you hardworking? 2. **Am / Is / Are** Mike tall? 3. **Am / Is / Are** I funny?	○ ○ ○

| | | | | Number Correct | 0 | 1 | 2 | 3 |

Skill	Circle the answer.	Is it correct?
B. Use possessive and plural nouns.	4. Her two **sister's / sisters** are pretty. 5. His **mother's / mothers** name is Ann. 6. My **brother's / brothers** are young.	○ ○ ○

| | | | | Number Correct | 0 | 1 | 2 | 3 |

Skill	Circle the answer.	Is it correct?
C. Describe people.	7. She's not shy. She's **tall / outgoing**. 8. We're not messy. We're **lazy / neat**. 9. They're not tall. They're **short / heavy**.	○ ○ ○

| | | | | Number Correct | 0 | 1 | 2 | 3 |

Skill	Circle the answer.	Is it correct?
D. Describe family members.	10. My mother's sister is my **aunt / daughter**. 11. My mother's mother is my **sister / grandmother**. 12. My aunt's husband is my **father / uncle**.	○ ○ ○

| | | | | Number Correct | 0 | 1 | 2 | 3 |

COUNT the number of correct answers above. Fill in the bubbles.

Chart Your Success				
Skill	Need more practice	Okay	Good	Excellent!
A. Ask yes/no questions with *be*.	⓪	①	②	③
B. Use possessive and plural nouns.	⓪	①	②	③
C. Describe people.	⓪	①	②	③
D. Describe family members.	⓪	①	②	③

LESSON 1: Grammar and Vocabulary

1 GRAMMAR PICTURE DICTIONARY. Listen and repeat.
TCD1, 33
SCD, 14
In my classroom . . .

1. There is **a map**.
2. There is **a clock**.
3. There are **many desks**.
4. There is **a table**.
5. There is **a computer**.
6. There are **three windows**.
7. There is **a pencil sharpener**.
8. There is **a trash can**.
9. There are **CDs**.
10. There is **a board**. — Welcome to Class!
11. There is **a copier**.
12. There are **many chairs**.

2 NOTICE THE GRAMMAR. Look at Activity 1. Underline *There is* or *There are*. Circle the plural words (the words that end in **s**).

There is and There are

Affirmative Statements

There	be	Noun	
There	is	a map	in the classroom.
	are	windows	

Negative Statements

There			
There	isn't	a teacher	in the classroom.
	aren't	any windows	

Yes/No Questions

Be	there	Noun
Is	there	a map?
Are		any windows?

Answers

		there	be
Yes,	there	is	
		are.	

		there	be
No,	there	isn't.	
		aren't.	

---

3 **WRITE.** Look at the picture. Complete the sentences. Use *is, isn't, are,* or *aren't.*

In the classroom, . . .

1. There ____is____ one map.
2. There _____ a clock.
3. There _____ three students.
4. There _____ three desks.
5. There _____ four chairs.
6. There _____ a copier.
7. There _____ a computer.
8. There _____ any CDs.

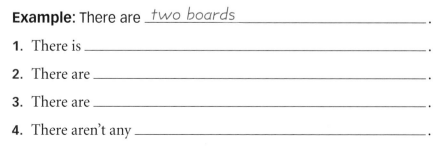

4 **WHAT ABOUT YOU?** Complete the sentences about *your* classroom.

Example: There are _two boards_____.

1. There is _____.
2. There are _____.
3. There are _____.
4. There aren't any _____.

LESSON 2: Grammar Practice Plus

1 WRITE words under the pictures. Use the words in the box.

| bag | backpack | book | cell phone | marker | notebook | pen | ~~pencil~~ |

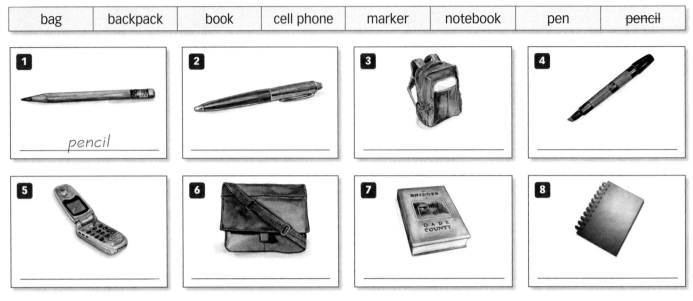

1 _____ pencil _____

2 _____

3 _____

4 _____

5 _____

6 _____

7 _____

8 _____

LISTEN and repeat. Are your answers correct?

2 WHAT ABOUT YOU? Look in your bag or backpack. Write the things you see.

There is...	There are...

TALK with a partner.

Are there any pens in your backpack?

Yes, there are three.

Math: Multiplication

Read the problems. Write the equations. Read the equations to a partner.

Problems	Equations
1. There are two classrooms. There are two computers in each classroom. How many computers are there?	2 x 2 = 4 Two times two equals four.
2. There are three backpacks. There are two notebooks in each backpack. How many notebooks are there?	_____ x _____ = _____
3. There are six classes. There are 20 students in each class. How many students are there?	_____ x _____ = _____

3 **TALK** about the picture.

There is a board. There are 11 notebooks.

NO CELL PHONES!

Paul

Elsa

Yen

David

Alex

Ana

Aziza

4 **LISTEN.** Answer the questions. Write the number.

TCD1, 35

1. ___16___   3. _____   5. _____   7. _____

2. _____   4. _____   6. _____   8. _____

5 **TALK** with a partner. Ask and answer questions about the things in the picture.

How many students are there?

There are 16 students.

Are there any cell phones?

Yes, there are ten.

LESSON 3: Listening and Conversation

1 **WRITE.** Complete the questions with *Is there* or *Are there*.

1 _____Is there_____ a meeting room?

2 _____ computer classes?

3 _____ DVDs?

4 _____ books in Spanish?

🎧 **LISTEN** and repeat. Are your answers correct?

TCD1, 36

🎧 **2** **LISTEN** and circle the letter.

TCD1, 37

1. A.   B.   C.

2. A.   B.   C.

3. A.   B.   C.

LISTEN AGAIN. Match the object and the location.

_____ **1.** DVDs   **a.** meeting room

_____ **2.** copier   **b.** desk

_____ **3.** backpack   **c.** table

3 LISTEN and read.

A: Hello. Washington School Library.

B: Hi. I have a question.

A: Yes?

B: Are there any computers in the library?

A: Yes. There are 20 computers.

B: Great. Thanks a lot.

LISTEN AGAIN and repeat. Then practice with a partner.

4 PRACTICE THE CONVERSATION with a partner.

1 copiers / 3

2 meeting rooms / 2

3 DVDs / more

4 CDs / 1,000 or more

5 computer classes / 1

6 books in Spanish / hundreds

5 TALK. Look at the website. Ask and answer questions with a partner.

The Midtown Library on Central Avenue offers:

- Thousands of books, videos, DVDs, and CDs
- 13 computers
- Materials in Spanish and Vietnamese. Two hundred books in each language, and magazines, videos, DVDs, and music CDs
- More than 20 books, tapes, and videos to learn English
- One class for beginning English and one for intermediate English
- A meeting room

Are there any computers?

Yes, there are 13.

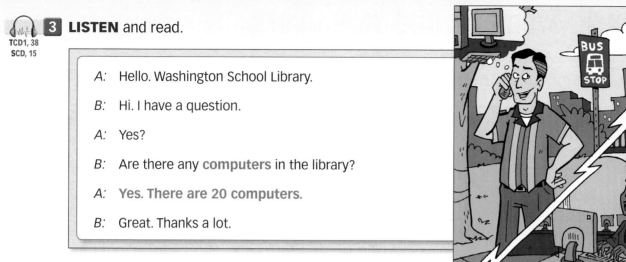

LESSON 4: Grammar and Vocabulary

1 GRAMMAR PICTURE DICTIONARY. Listen and repeat.

1. The **lobby** is on the first floor.

2. The **stairs** are over there.

3. The **elevator** is in the **lobby**.

4. The **water fountain** is in the snack bar.

5. The **snack bar** is in the Harper building.

6. The **vending machine** is in the hall.

7. The **restrooms** are on the first floor.

8. The **office** is on the second floor.

9. The **public telephones** are in the office.

2 NOTICE THE GRAMMAR. Look at Activity 1. Circle *in* and *on*.

| Use prepositions to locate places at school.

Prepositions of Location

We use prepositions to tell locations.

We use *at* with addresses and *home, school,* and *work.*

	Preposition	
There is an office	at	42 Pine Street.
		school.

We use *in* with names of buildings or rooms.

The snack bar is	in	room 206.
		the Harper Building.

We use *on* with floors of a building or streets.

The library is	on	the second floor.
		Main Street.

---

3 **WRITE.** Complete the sentences. Use *in, on,* or *at.*

1. The water fountain is ___*in*___ the hall.

2. The restrooms are _____ the first floor.

3. The vending machines are _____ the second floor.

4. The snack bar is _____ the Blake Building.

5. The office is _____ room 102.

6. Hannah is _____ school.

7. She is _____ the office.

8. We are _____ 130 Broad Street. Where are you?

4 **WHAT ABOUT YOU?** Complete the sentences about your school. Use *in, on,* or *at.*

1. The water fountain is _____.

2. The restrooms are _____.

3. The vending machines are _____.

4. The public telephone is _____.

5. (Your idea) _____.

TALK. Read your sentences to a partner.

LESSON 5: Grammar Practice Plus

1 **WRITE.** Complete the sentences. Use the words in the box.

computer lab	information desk	library	security office

1

The _____ is on the first floor.

2

The _____ is at 521 Fifth Street.

3

The _____ is on Fifth Street.

4

The _____ is in Room 102.

LISTEN and repeat. Are your answers correct?

TCD1, 40

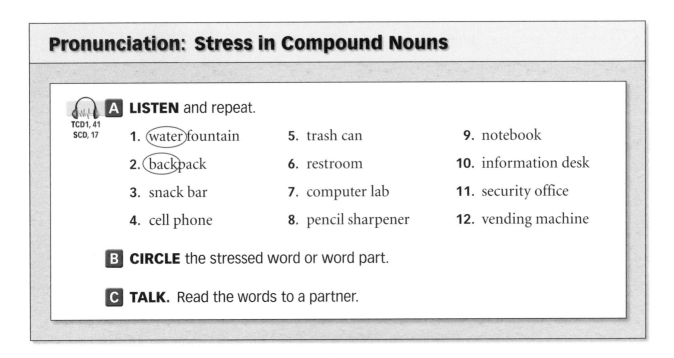

Pronunciation: Stress in Compound Nouns

A **LISTEN** and repeat.

TCD1, 41
SCD, 17

1. (water) fountain
2. (back) pack
3. snack bar
4. cell phone

5. trash can
6. restroom
7. computer lab
8. pencil sharpener

9. notebook
10. information desk
11. security office
12. vending machine

B **CIRCLE** the stressed word or word part.

C **TALK.** Read the words to a partner.

Read a map of a school. • Describe locations at school.

2 **MATCH.** Look at the map. Match the questions and answers.

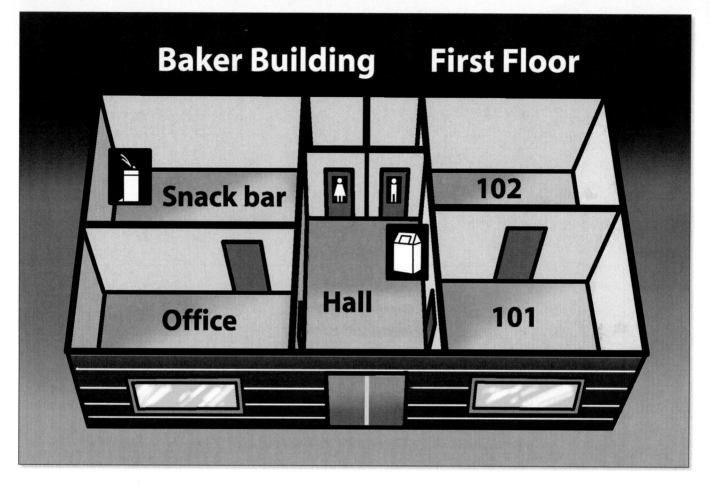

___a___ **1.** Where is the trash can?

_____ **2.** Is room 101 on the first floor?

_____ **3.** Where is the office?

_____ **4.** Are there any restrooms?

_____ **5.** Where is the water fountain?

a. It's in the hall.

b. It's on the first floor.

c. Yes, there are. On the first floor.

d. It's in the snack bar.

e. Yes, it is.

TALK. Ask and answer the questions with a partner.

3 **GAME.** Think of a place or a thing in your school. Say the location. Your partner guesses.

They're on the second floor. They're in the hall.

The vending machines?

LESSON 6: Apply Your Knowledge

1 **READ** the sign. Write the places on the map.

Welcome to Washington School!

Information Desk......................First floor — Main Hall
Security Office..........................Room 101
Library......................................Room 203
Computer Lab ....Room 102
Snack Bar ....Room 103

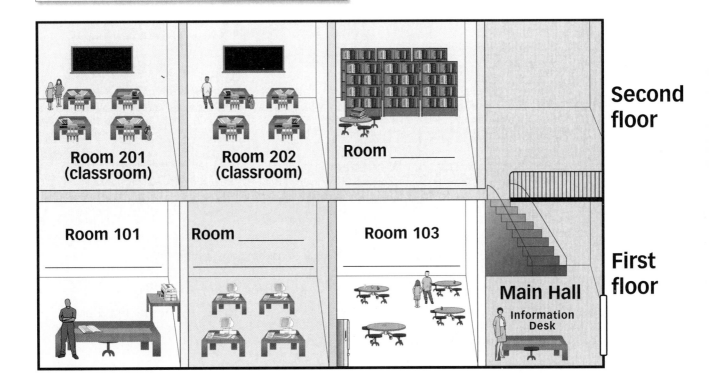

Room 201
(classroom)

Room 202
(classroom)

Room _____

Second floor

Room 101
_____

Room _____

Room 103

Main Hall
Information Desk

First floor

TCD1, 42

2 **LISTEN.** Write the location.

	Location
1. vending machines	*in the snack bar*
2. student books	
3. restrooms	

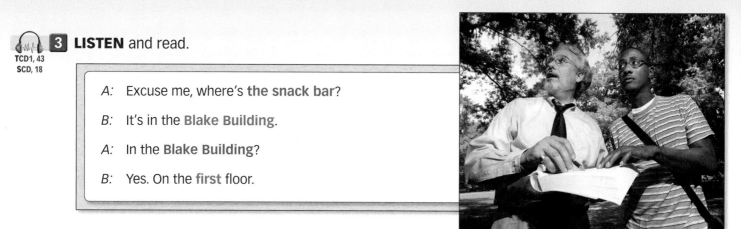

3 LISTEN and read.

A: Excuse me, where's **the snack bar**?

B: It's in the **Blake Building**.

A: In the **Blake Building**?

B: Yes. On the **first** floor.

LISTEN AGAIN and repeat. Then practice with a partner.

4 PRACTICE THE CONVERSATION with a partner.
Ask about the places in the picture.

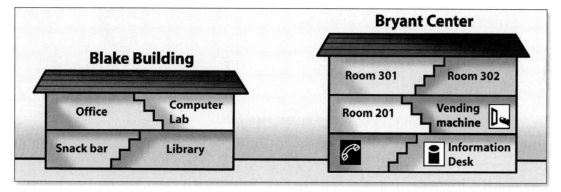

5 WHAT ABOUT YOU? Complete the sign with information about your school.

Welcome to _____
(name of school)

Vending machines _____

Restrooms _____

Public telephones _____

Computer lab _____

_____
(your idea)

TALK. Work with a partner. Ask about places at your school.

Where are the vending machines?

They're on the second floor.

LESSON 7: Reading

1 THINK ABOUT IT. What classes are there at your school?

2 BEFORE YOU READ. Look at the Web site. What is the reading about? Check ☑.

☐ family ☐ school ☐ students

> **Reading Tip**
> Take notes on a diagram. This helps you understand a reading.

3 READ. Take notes on the diagram.

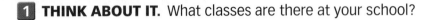

Winter Valley School

- Home
- Register
- Classes
- About Us
- Career

Winter Valley is a very big school. There are more than 150 classes, including classes in English, computers, and math. There are 10,000 students at Winter Valley School, from 30 different countries. Classes are offered at three locations: Center City, North Campus, and West Campus. There is a snack bar, bookstore, computer lab, and library at each location.

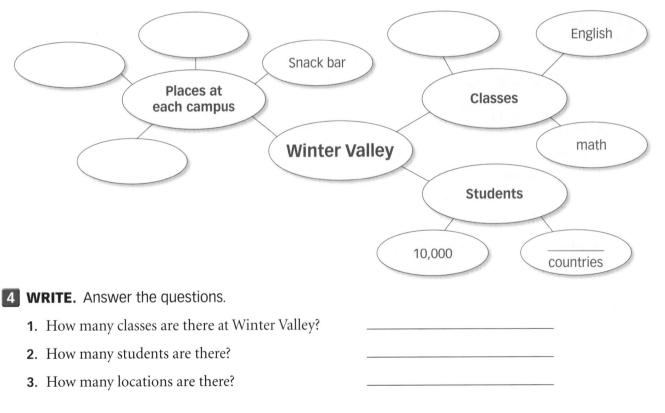

4 WRITE. Answer the questions.

1. How many classes are there at Winter Valley? _____

2. How many students are there? _____

3. How many locations are there? _____

Read a website. • Use correct punctuation.

Writing

1 EDIT. Add a period at the end of each sentence.

My School

My school is in San Francisco. There is a library and a snack bar at my school My classroom is on the first floor There are 24 desks in my classroom There is also a table Two computers are on the table There are 21 students in the class Seven students are from Mexico, two are from Honduras, five are from Vietnam, four are from Russia, and three are from Somalia There are books and notebooks for all the students

2 WRITE. Answer the questions about your school and class. Use complete sentences.

1. What city is your school in?

   My school is in _____

2. What places or things are there at your school?

   _____

3. What is in your classroom?

   There are _____ in my classroom.

4. How many students are there?

   _____

5. What countries are the students from?

   _____

6. How many students are from each country?

   _____

3 EDIT your sentences.

☐ Is there a capital letter?

☐ Is there a period?

Career Connection

1 **READ** and listen. Then practice with a partner.

TCD1, 44

Panel 1: Here's the supply room.

Panel 2: And here's the break room.

Panel 3: There's a problem with your new office, Laura. / What's wrong?

Panel 4: Look.

2 **WRITE.** Look at Laura's office. What things are good? What things are bad? Complete the chart.

Good things	Bad things
There is a big table.	

3 **WHAT ABOUT YOU?** What is in the perfect office for you? Talk to a partner.

Match personal characteristics to jobs.

Check Your Progress!

Skill	Circle the answer.	Is it correct?
A. Use *there is/there are*.	1. **There is / There are** two desks in the office. 2. **Is there / Are there** any restrooms in this building? 3. No, **there aren't. / No, there not.**	☐ ☐ ☐

		Number Correct	0	1	2	3

Skill		Is it correct?
B. Use prepositions of location.	4. The snack bar is **in / on** the first floor. 5. Our office is **in / at** 321 South Street. 6. The vending machines are **in / on** the snack bar.	☐ ☐ ☐

		Number Correct	0	1	2	3

Skill		Is it correct?
C. Talk about classroom things.	7. There are two **pens / desks** in my backpack. 8. There is a **cell phone / window** in my bag. 9. Write with the **pencil / clock**.	☐ ☐ ☐

		Number Correct	0	1	2	3

Skill		Is it correct?
D. Talk about school places.	10. There are books in the **elevator / library**. 11. The **vending machines / computers** are in the snack bar. 12. The information desk is in the **lobby / restroom**.	☐ ☐ ☐

		Number Correct	0	1	2	3

COUNT the number of correct answers above. Fill in the bubbles.

Chart Your Success				
Skill	Need more practice	Okay	Good	Excellent!
A. Use *there is/there are*.	⓪	①	②	③
B. Use prepositions of location.	⓪	①	②	③
C. Talk about classroom things.	⓪	①	②	③
D. Talk about school places.	⓪	①	②	③

LESSON 1: Grammar and Vocabulary

1 GRAMMAR PICTURE DICTIONARY. Listen and repeat.

TCD2, 2
SCD, 19

How's the Weather?

1 It's <u>hot</u>.

2 It's **sunny**.

3 It's **humid**.

4 It's **warm**.

5 It's **clear**.

6 It's **foggy**.

7 It's **cool**.

8 It's **cloudy**.

9 It's **rainy**.

10 It's **cold**.

11 It's **windy**.

12 It's **snowy**.

2 NOTICE THE GRAMMAR. Look at Activity 1. Circle *It's*. Underline the weather words.

It's with Weather

We use *It's* to talk about weather.

Affirmative Statements

It's	hot. sunny.

Negative Statements

It's	not	cold. rainy.

Questions

Is	it	cold? rainy?

Answers

Yes,	it	is.	No,	it	isn't.

---

3 WRITE. Look at the pictures. Complete the sentences with weather words.

1. It's _____ rainy _____ .
2. It's _____ .
3. It's not _____ .
4. It's not _____ .

5. It's _____ sunny _____ .
6. It's _____ .
7. It's not _____ .
8. It's not _____ .

---

4 WHAT ABOUT YOU? Talk to a partner. How's the weather today in your city?

1. Is it cool?
2. Is it rainy?
3. Is it windy?

4. Is it humid?
5. Is it foggy?
6. Is it clear?

Is it cool today?

No, it isn't. It's warm.

LESSON 2: Grammar Practice Plus

1 **WRITE.** Complete the sentences. Use the words in the box.

cold	cool	hot	windy

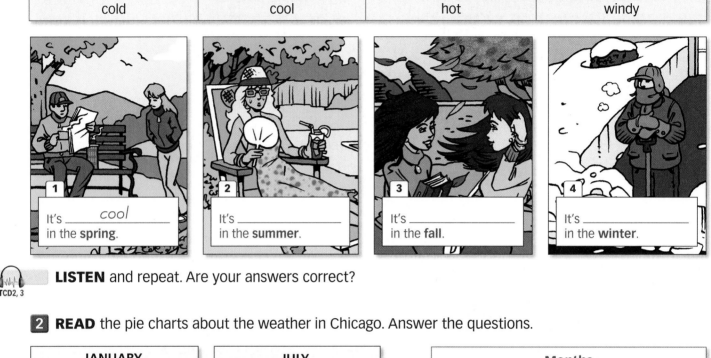

1 It's ____cool____ in the **spring**.

2 It's _____ in the **summer**.

3 It's _____ in the **fall**.

4 It's _____ in the **winter**.

🎧 TCD2, 3   **LISTEN** and repeat. Are your answers correct?

2 **READ** the pie charts about the weather in Chicago. Answer the questions.

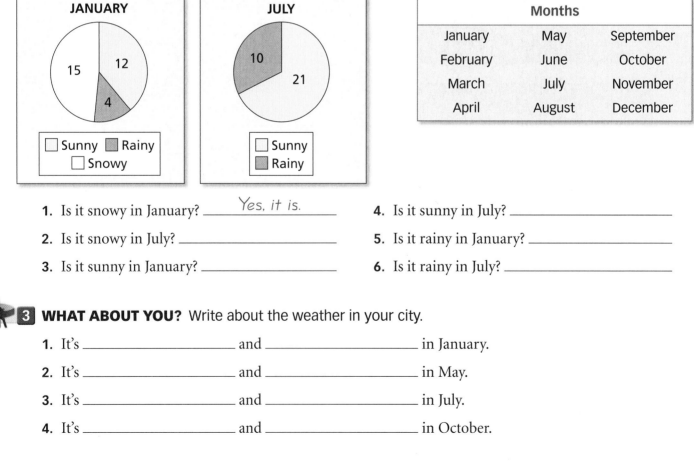

JANUARY

15   12   4

☐ Sunny ■ Rainy
☐ Snowy

JULY

10   21

☐ Sunny
■ Rainy

Months		
January	May	September
February	June	October
March	July	November
April	August	December

1. Is it snowy in January? ___Yes, it is.___

2. Is it snowy in July? _____

3. Is it sunny in January? _____

4. Is it sunny in July? _____

5. Is it rainy in January? _____

6. Is it rainy in July? _____

3 **WHAT ABOUT YOU?** Write about the weather in your city.

1. It's _____ and _____ in January.

2. It's _____ and _____ in May.

3. It's _____ and _____ in July.

4. It's _____ and _____ in October.

Read a pie chart. • Describe weather and seasons.

4 **TALK** about the pictures.

5 **LISTEN.** Number the pictures.

LISTEN AGAIN. Complete the sentence with a season.

1. It's _____winter_____ in London.   3. It's _____ in Chicago.

2. It's _____ in Mexico City.   4. It's _____ in Bogotá.

6 **TALK** to a partner. Ask about the weather in London, Mexico City, and Bogotá.

LESSON 3: Listening and Conversation

1 **LISTEN** to the weather report. Look at the map and circle the correct city.

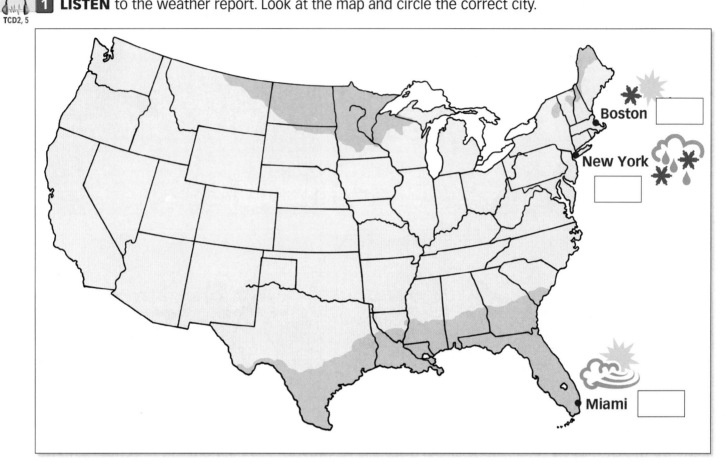

Boston

New York

Miami

LISTEN AGAIN. On the map, write the temperature in each city.

Math: Temperatures

Match the temperatures.

Celsius	Fahrenheit
_b_ **1.** 11	**a.** 95
___ **2.** 26	**b.** 52
___ **3.** 35	**c.** 41
___ **4.** 5	**d.** 78

°F °C

Understand a weather report. • Understand Celsius and Fahrenheit temperatures.

2 **LISTEN** and read.

> A: Hi! How's the weather in **Rio de Janiero**?
>
> B: It's **hot**. It's **85°**. How's the weather in **Seattle**?
>
> A: It's **cool** and **rainy**. It's **49°**.

LISTEN AGAIN and repeat. Then practice with a partner.

3 **PRACTICE THE CONVERSATION** with a partner.

4 **WRITE.** Choose a city. Write a weather report. Read the report to your classmates.

Good morning, _____!
                    (city)

Today is _____ .
              (date)

It's _____ degrees.
       (temperature)

It's _____ and _____ .
        (weather)   (weather)

LESSON 4: Grammar and Vocabulary

TCD2, 7
SCD, 21

1 **GRAMMAR PICTURE DICTIONARY.** Listen and repeat.

What time is it?

1. It's **two o'clock**.
2. It's **two oh five**.
3. It's **two fifteen**.
4. It's **two-twenty**.
5. It's **two-thirty**.
6. It's **two-forty-five**.

When is your class?

7. It's **in the morning**.
8. It's **in the afternoon**.
9. It's **in the evening**.
10. It's **at night**.

2 **NOTICE THE GRAMMAR.** Look at Activity 1. Circle *What time* and *When*. Underline *is*.

Ask about and tell the time. • Ask and answer information questions with *be*.

What Time and When Questions with Be

Questions			**Answers**

Question Word	*be*	Noun	
What time	is	it?	It's 9:30 A.M. It's 12:00 noon.
What time	is	your English class?	It's at 9:00 A.M.
When	are	the classes?	They're at 2:00 P.M. and 3:00 P.M.
When	is	your birthday?	It's in November.
	are	your classes?	They're in the morning.

3 **WRITE.** Put the questions in order. Then write the answers.

Questions

Answers

1. Eva's birthday? / is / When

   When is Eva's birthday?   April *It's in April.*

2. is / What time / the test?

   _____   10:30 _____

3. is / When / the first day of class?

   _____   September 3rd _____

4. is / the English class? / What time

   _____   4:00 _____

5. When / their birthdays? / are

   _____   May _____

TALK. Practice the questions and answers with a partner.

4 **WHAT ABOUT YOU?** Write your answers.

1. What time is it now? _____ .

2. When is your birthday? _____ .

3. What time is your English class? _____ .

TALK. Ask and answer the questions with a partner.

LESSON 5: Grammar Practice Plus

> We use **on** with dates.
> Example: My birthday is **on** November 15th.

1 WRITE. Complete the conversations. Write the month.

1
A: When is **New Year's Day**?
B: It's on _January_ 1st.

2
A: When is **Valentine's Day**?
B: It's on _____ 14th.

3
A: When is **Independence Day**?
B: It's on _____ 4th.

4
A: A: When is **Labor Day**?
B: It's in _____.

5
A: When is **Halloween**?
B: It's on _____ 31st.

6
A: When is **Thanksgiving**?
B: It's in _____.

TCD2, 8   **LISTEN** and repeat. Are your answers correct?

Pronunciation: Ordinal Numbers

TCD2, 9
SCD, 22   **A LISTEN** and repeat.

1st first	6th sixth	11th eleventh	16th sixteenth	21st twenty-first
2nd second	7th seventh	12th twelfth	17th seventeenth	30th thirtieth
3rd third	8th eighth	13th thirteenth	18th eighteenth	31st thirty-first
4th fourth	9th ninth	14th fourteenth	19th nineteenth	
5th fifth	10th tenth	15th fifteenth	20th twentieth	

TCD2, 10
SCD, 23   **B LISTEN** to the sentences. Check ☑ the word you hear.

1. ☐ fifteen   ☐ fifteenth   3. ☐ thirty ☐ thirtieth   5. ☐ twelve ☐ twelfth

2. ☐ twenty-one ☐ twenty-first   4. ☐ four   ☐ fourth   6. ☐ nine   ☐ ninth

C TALK with a partner. Say one word from each pair of words in B.
Your partner listens and circles the word.

2 **WRITE** the words in the chart.

> Remember:
> in = seasons, months, years
> on = dates
> at = times.

~~2008~~	9:15 A.M.	July 4	February	December 2
Summer	January 15	May	7:45 P.M.	Winter

in	on	at
2008		

3 **WRITE.** Complete the sentences. Use *in*, *on*, or *at*.

1. My class is __at__ 10:00 A.M.

2. It's humid _____ the summer.

3. My birthday is _____ February 6th.

4. My sister's birthday is _____ February.

5. It's foggy _____ the spring.

6. New Year's Day is _____ January 1st.

7. The movie is _____ 8:15 P.M.

8. Independence Day is _____ July 4th.

4 **TALK** with three classmates. Complete the chart.

Where are you from?

I'm from Colombia.

When is your birthday?

It's on June 19.

How's the weather on your birthday in Colombia?

It's hot and humid.

	Classmate's Name	Country	Date	Weather
Example:	Eduardo	Colombia	June 19	hot, humid
1.				
2.				
3.				

LESSON 6: Apply Your Knowledge

1 READ the list of important school dates. Circle the dates with no classes.

Important School Year Dates
Days with NO CLASSES in blue

Registration	August 25–29	Exams	December 16–18
First Day of Class	August 31	Winter Break	December 18–January 3
Labor Day	(September 4)	First Day of Class	January 4
New Student Meeting	September 7, 7:00 P.M.	Valentine's Day Party	February 14, 4:00 P.M.
Teacher Workday	October 16	Spring Break	March 12–16
Halloween Party	October 31, 8:00 P.M.	Last Day of Class	May 25
Thanksgiving	November 23	Exams	May 27–29
Last Day of Class	December 15		

2 CIRCLE the correct letter.

1. Are there classes on Halloween?

A. Yes, there are.   **B.** No, there aren't.   **C.** I don't know.

2. What time is the New Student Meeting?

A. in October   **B.** on September 7   **C.** at 7:00 P.M.

3. When is Thanksgiving?

A. at 7:00 P.M.   **B.** on November 23   **C.** on October 16

3 LISTEN to the conversations. Complete the calendar.

TCD2, 11–13

Ashville Community School • 1275 Baker Avenue 555-0045
September Schedule

August 31	First day of class, 10:00 A.M. Teacher: Mr. Brown
September	Labor day, No Class
7	New Student Meeting, P.M. Room 410

4 **LISTEN** and read.

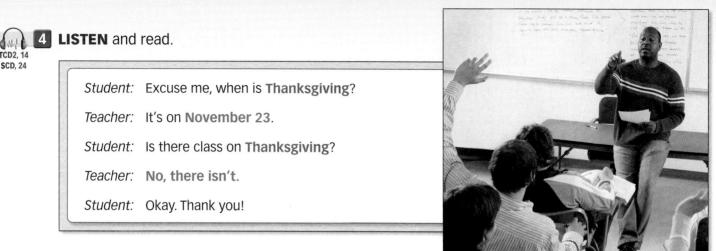

Student: Excuse me, when is **Thanksgiving**?

Teacher: It's on **November 23**.

Student: Is there class on **Thanksgiving**?

Teacher: **No, there isn't**.

Student: Okay. Thank you!

LISTEN AGAIN and repeat. Then practice with a partner.

5 **PRACTICE THE CONVERSATION** with a partner. Use the list of dates on page 64.

1. Halloween
2. New Year's Day
3. Labor Day
4. Valentine's Day

6 **PUT IT TOGETHER.** Work in a small group. Make a school calendar for a new school.

Example:

> ### Elena's School for Busy Actors
> 1422 11th Avenue   (312) 555-9422
>
> **Class Times:** Mondays 9 P.M., Tuesdays 8 P.M.
> **Teacher(s):** Antonio Banderas
> **First Day of Class:** February 4
> **Last Day of Class:** July 12
> **Holidays (No Class):** Valentine's Day, Independence Day

LESSON 7: Reading

1 THINK ABOUT IT. Write an email address you know. Who is it for?

_____

2 BEFORE YOU READ. Look at the email. Circle the words from the box.

| TO | FROM | DATE | SUBJECT |

Reading Tip

Look for important details before you read.

3 READ the email. What season is it?

From: ryan_k@studentmail.net

To: mike_p@collegemail.net

Date: December 29, 7:41 P.M.

Subject: Hi from New York!

Hi Mike,

Hi! How are you? I'm in New York! I'm with my brother, Joshua. It's winter break, so there aren't any classes this week. It's cold in New York… It's snowy and windy too.

Where are you? Are you on winter break? When is your first day of class? My first day of class is on January 10. Talk to you soon!

Bye,

Ryan

4 CIRCLE the correct letter.

1. Who is the email from? **A.** Ryan **B.** Joshua **C.** Mike

2. Where is Ryan? **A.** in New York **B.** in school **C.** at home

3. How is the weather? **A.** sunny **B.** rainy **C.** snowy

4. When is Ryan's first day of class? **A.** December 29 **B.** January 1 **C.** January 10

Understand and write an email message.

Writing

1 MATCH. Look at the email on page 66. Match the information.

_d_	**1.** TO	**a.**	Hi from New York!
_____	**2.** FROM	**b.**	December 29, 2008
_____	**3.** DATE	**c.**	ryan_k@studentmail.net
_____	**4.** TIME	~~**d.** mike_p@collegemail.net~~
_____	**5.** SUBJECT	**e.**	7:41 P.M.

2 WRITE. You're on vacation. You're going to write an email to a friend or family member. Write the information for your email.

TO:	
FROM:	
DATE:	
TIME:	
SUBJECT:	

3 WRITE your email.

> **Writing Tip**
>
> For email messages:
> 1. Write a subject line.
> 2. Check capital and lower case letters.
> 3. Check the spelling of email addresses.

From: _____

To: _____

Date: _____

Subject: _____

Hi _____ ,
_____(name)_____

How are you? It's _____ , and there are no classes. I'm on
_____(holiday)_____

vacation. I'm in _____ . It's _____ . The
_____(city)_____   _____(season)_____

weather is _____ . It's _____ and
_____(good / bad)_____   _____(weather)_____

_____ . See you soon!
_____(weather)_____

Bye,

_____
_____(your name)_____

Career Connection

1 **READ** and listen.

2 **TALK.** Answer the questions.

1. What is the holiday?
2. What time is it?
3. Where are Isabel and Tom?
4. What is the problem?

3 **WHAT ABOUT YOU?** Are there holidays at your school or your job? Make a list. Then read your list to a partner.

Check Your Progress!

Skill	Circle the answer.	Is it correct?
A. Describe weather and seasons.	1. It's spring. It's cloudy and **rainy** / **sunny**. 2. It's summer. It's humid and **hot** / **dry**. 3. It's winter. It's snowy and **cool** / **cold**.	☐ ☐ ☐

	Number Correct	0	1	2	3

Skill	Circle the answer.	Is it correct?
B. Use *in*, *on*, and *at*.	4. It's hot **in** / **on** summer. 5. The class is **on** / **at** 2:00 P.M. 6. My birthday is **on** / **in** Tuesday.	☐ ☐ ☐

	Number Correct	0	1	2	3

Skill	Circle the answer.	Is it correct?
C. Ask questions with *What time* and *When*.	7. **What time** / **When** is it? It's 4:45 P.M. 8. **What time** / **When** is your birthday? It's in April. 9. **What time** / **When** are the classes? They're in the morning.	☐ ☐ ☐

	Number Correct	0	1	2	3

Skill	Circle the answer.	Is it correct?
D. Describe holidays.	10. New Year's Day is in **December** / **January**. 11. Independence Day is in **June** / **July**. 12. Thanksgiving is in **October** / **November**.	☐ ☐ ☐

	Number Correct	0	1	2	3

COUNT the number of correct answers above. Fill in the bubbles.

Chart Your Success				
Skill	Need more practice	Okay	Good	Excellent!
A. Describe weather and seasons.	⓪	①	②	③
B. Use *in*, *on*, and *at*.	⓪	①	②	③
C. Ask questions with *What time* and *When*.	⓪	①	②	③
D. Describe holidays.	⓪	①	②	③

LESSON 1: Grammar and Vocabulary

1 **GRAMMAR PICTURE DICTIONARY.** Listen and repeat.

TCD2, 16
SCD, 25

Where's the …?

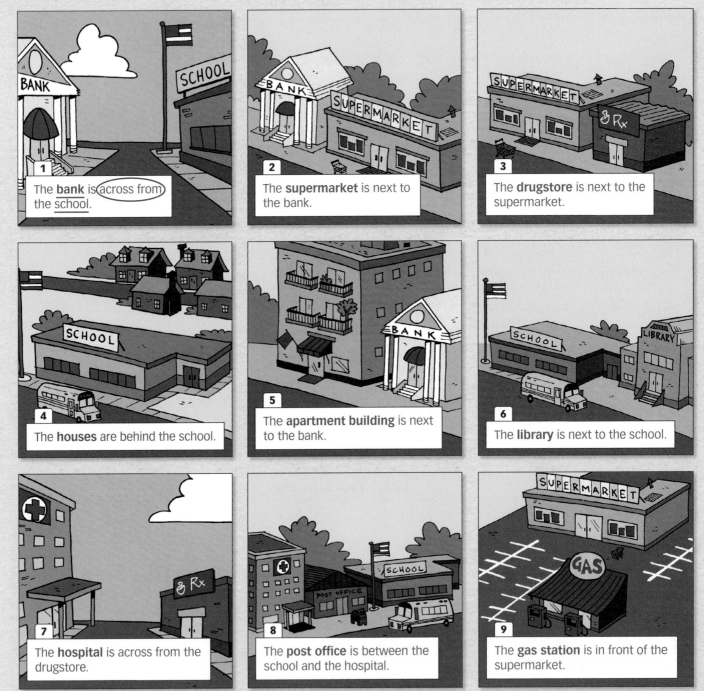

1 The **bank** is across from the school.

2 The **supermarket** is next to the bank.

3 The **drugstore** is next to the supermarket.

4 The **houses** are behind the school.

5 The **apartment building** is next to the bank.

6 The **library** is next to the school.

7 The **hospital** is across from the drugstore.

8 The **post office** is between the school and the hospital.

9 The **gas station** is in front of the supermarket.

2 **NOTICE THE GRAMMAR.** Look at Activity 1. Underline the places. Circle the prepositions.

Prepositions of Location, Part 2

We use prepositions to tell locations.

| 1 across from | 2 next to | 3 in front of | 4 behind | 5 between |

Noun	*be*	Preposition	Noun(s)
The bank		next to	the supermarket.
The library	is	between	the school and the post office.
The school		across from	the drugstore.
The houses	are	behind	the school.
The students		in front of	the school.

3 **WRITE.** Look at the picture. Write the correct preposition.

1. The bank is ___next to___ the apartment building.

2. The gas station is _____ the drugstore and the bank.

3. The drugstore is _____ the gas station.

4. The supermarket is _____ the gas station.

5. The bank is _____ the gas station and the apartment building.

4 **WHAT ABOUT YOU?** Write sentences about you. Use prepositions and your classmates' names.

Example: I am sitting ___between Ming and Edgar___.

1. I am sitting _____.

2. I am sitting _____.

3. I am sitting _____.

LESSON 2: Grammar Practice Plus

1 **LISTEN** and repeat.

| 1 hotel | 2 movie theater | 3 restaurant |
| 4 police station | 5 fire station | 6 community center |

2 **WRITE.** Match the occupations and the workplaces. Write words from the box in the chart.

| hospital | housekeeper | ~~police station~~ | restaurant | sales clerk |

Occupations	Workplaces
1. police officer	*police station*
2.	supermarket
3. server	
4. doctor	
5.	hotel

3 **WHAT ABOUT YOU?** Choose a place in your city. Complete the sentences.

Example: _My daughter's school is next to a bank._

1. _____ is next to _____.
             (place)

2. It's across from _____.

3. It's _____.

4. _____.

4 **TALK** about the picture.

The doctors are in front of the hospital.

5 **LISTEN.** Number the places in the picture.

TCD2, 18

6 **TALK** with a partner. Ask about the places.

1. bank
2. community center
3. fire station
4. hotel
5. movie theater

Where's the bank?

It's next to the post office.

LESSON 3: Listening and Conversation

1 **LISTEN.** Circle the correct letter.

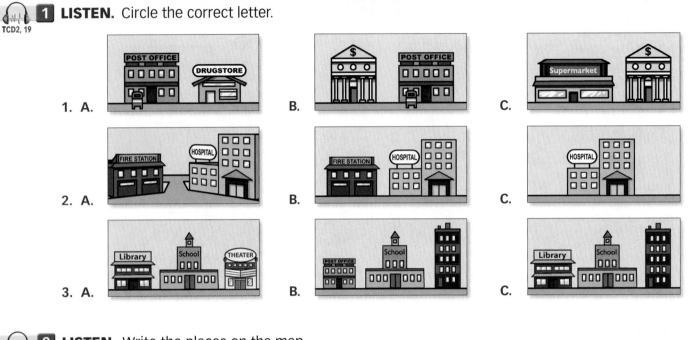

1. A.   B.   C.

2. A.   B.   C.

3. A.   B.   C.

2 **LISTEN.** Write the places on the map.

post office	movie theater	bank	supermarket	community center	fire station

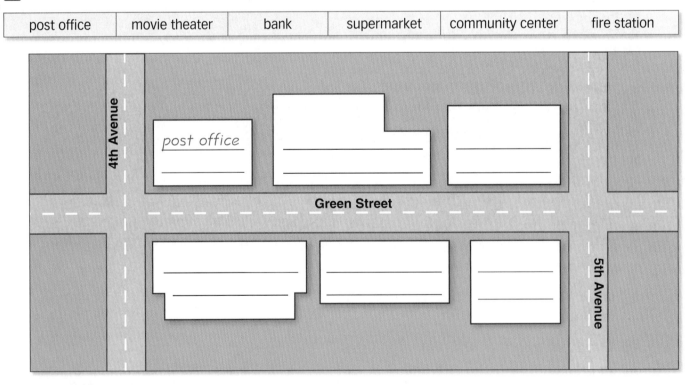

LISTEN AGAIN. Are your answers correct?

Ask and tell about locations. • Use a map.

3 **LISTEN** and read.

A: Excuse me. Where's the **post office**?

B: It's **next to** the **school**.

A: Oh…where's the **school**?

B: It's on **4ᵗʰ street**.

A: Okay. Thank you!

B: You're welcome!

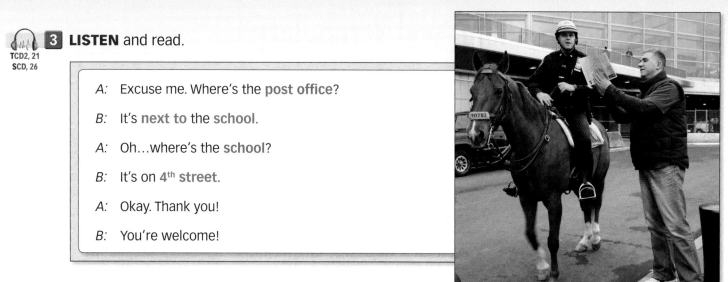

LISTEN AGAIN and repeat. Then practice with a partner.

4 **PRACTICE THE CONVERSATION** with a partner.

1	community center
2	hospital
3	bank
4	gas station

5 **WHAT ABOUT YOU?** Talk to a partner about the places in the box.

What's your favorite supermarket?

Super Food World.

Oh, where's that?

It's on Third Avenue.

Places
Supermarket
Movie Theater
Restaurant
Drugstore

LESSON 4: Grammar and Vocabulary

TCD2, 22
SCD, 27

1 GRAMMAR PICTURE DICTIONARY. Listen and repeat.

How do I get to your apartment?

1 (Start) on Main Street.

2 **Turn left** on 1st Avenue.

3 **Turn right** on Broadway.

4 **Go straight** on Broadway.

5 **Don't stop** in front of the apartment building.

6 **Make a U-turn.**

7 **Park** next to the police station.

8 **Cross** the street.

9 **Enter** the building and go to the third floor.

2 NOTICE THE GRAMMAR. Look at Activity 1. (Circle) the verbs.

Use imperatives to give directions.

Imperatives

There is no subject (*I, you, she*) in imperatives.

We use imperatives to give directions.

Affirmative Imperatives

Verb	
Turn	left on 1st Avenue.
Go	straight on Broadway.
Cross	the street.

Negative Imperatives

Do + not (Don't)	Verb	
Don't	turn	on 2nd Avenue.
Don't	go	on Jordan Road.
Don't	cross	the street.

3 **WRITE.** Complete the sentences. Use the words in the box.

Turn	Stop	~~Start~~	Park	Go

1. _____*Start*_____ on Johnson Road.

2. _____ left on Smith Street.

3. _____ straight.

4. _____ in front of the drugstore.

5. _____ between the drugstore and the restaurant.

LESSON 5: Grammar Practice Plus

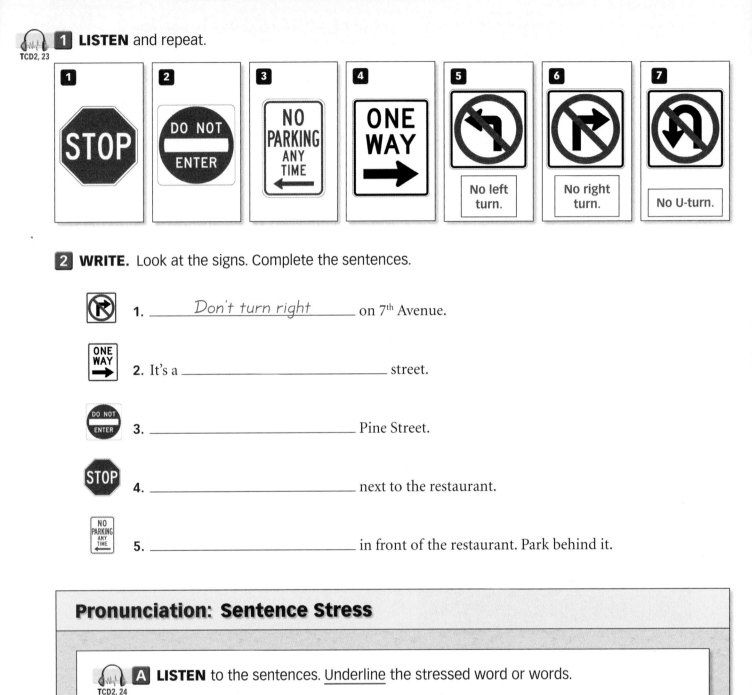

1 LISTEN and repeat.

TCD2, 23

1	2	3	4	5	6	7
STOP	DO NOT ENTER	NO PARKING ANY TIME	ONE WAY	No left turn.	No right turn.	No U-turn.

2 WRITE. Look at the signs. Complete the sentences.

1. ___*Don't turn right*___ on 7th Avenue.

2. It's a _____ street.

3. _____ Pine Street.

4. _____ next to the restaurant.

5. _____ in front of the restaurant. Park behind it.

Pronunciation: Sentence Stress

A LISTEN to the sentences. Underline the stressed word or words.

TCD2, 24
SCD, 28

1. Turn <u>right</u> on 2nd Avenue.
2. Stop in front of the store.
3. Go straight on Oak Lane.

4. Cross the street.
5. Park next to the police station.
6. Turn left on Johnson Road.

B LISTEN AGAIN and repeat. Then practice with a partner.

TCD2, 25
SCD, 29

3 LISTEN to the directions. Number the sentences in the correct order.

Go straight on Broadway. Then . . .

_____ Don't go on 4th Avenue. It's a one-way street.

__*1*__ Turn left on 6th Avenue. Don't turn right.

_____ Stop at E Street in front of the apartment building.

_____ Do not enter on Sherman Drive.

_____ Don't park on the street. Go behind the apartment building.

4 READ the directions. Look at the map. Circle the incorrect words in the directions.

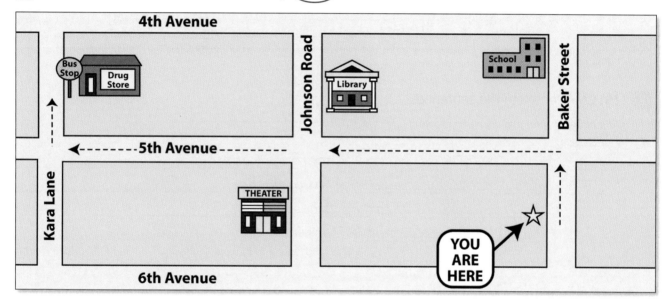

To get to the bus stop . . .

1. Go straight on Main Street.

2. Turn right on 5th Avenue.

3. Don't cross Johnson Road.

4. Turn left on Kara Lane.

5. Stop in front of the bank.

WRITE the directions again. Correct the words.

To get to the bus stop . . .

1. *Go straight on Baker Street.* _____

2. _____

3. _____

4. _____

5. _____

LESSON 6: Apply Your Knowledge

1 **READ.** Look at the map. Circle the street names.

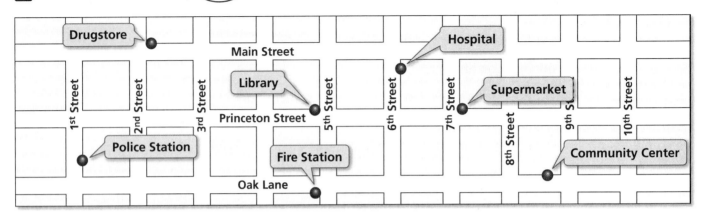

2 **LISTEN.** Complete the sentences.

TCD2, 27

1. ___Turn right___ on Princeton Street.
2. Go _____ for two blocks.
3. _____ at 1st Street.
4. _____ on 5th Street.
5. _____ on the street in front of the _____.

Math: Calculate Distance

A **WRITE.** Look at the map above. Calculate the distances.

1. From the drugstore to the hospital = ___5___ blocks

2. From the police station to the fire station = _____ blocks

3. From the supermarket to the library = _____ blocks

4. From the library to the drugstore = _____ blocks

B **TALK** with a partner about your answers.

How far is it from the drugstore to the hospital?

It's four blocks.

| Calculate distance using a map.

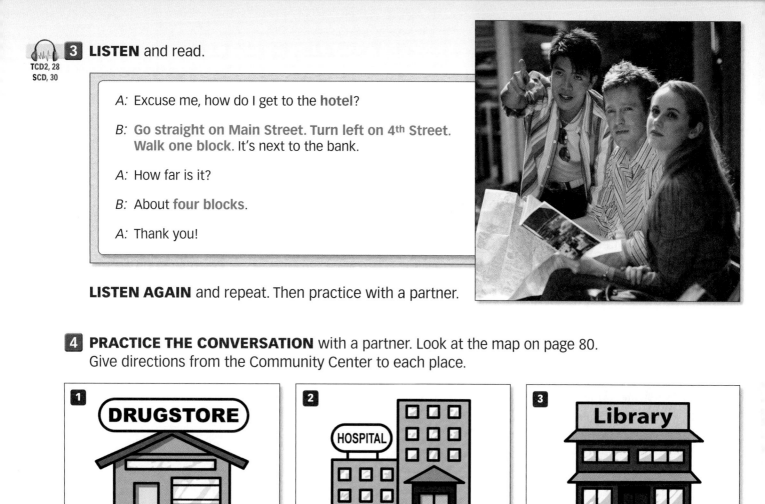

3 **LISTEN** and read.

TCD2, 28
SCD, 30

> *A:* Excuse me, how do I get to the **hotel**?
>
> *B:* **Go straight on Main Street. Turn left on 4th Street. Walk one block.** It's next to the bank.
>
> *A:* How far is it?
>
> *B:* About **four blocks**.
>
> *A:* Thank you!

LISTEN AGAIN and repeat. Then practice with a partner.

4 **PRACTICE THE CONVERSATION** with a partner. Look at the map on page 80. Give directions from the Community Center to each place.

1 DRUGSTORE

2 HOSPITAL

3 Library

4 Police Station

5 FIRE STATION

6 Supermarket

5 **WRITE.** Look at the map on page 80. Choose two places. Draw a line from one place to the other place. Then write directions.

1. Start on _____ Street.

2. Turn _____ on _____.

3. _____.

4. _____.

TALK. Read your directions to a classmate. Where are you?

LESSON 7: Reading

1 **THINK ABOUT IT.** What public places are there in your community? Check ☑ the places.

☐ police station   ☐ fire station   ☐ community center

☐ hospital   ☐ library   ☐ school

2 **BEFORE YOU READ.** What public places are there in Madison? Look at the brochure. Make a list: _community center_

Reading Tip
Before you read, look for headings. Headings are in dark letters: **Community Center**.

3 **READ** the brochure. Underline the words for streets and places in the community.

Welcome To Madison!
There are many government services in Madison.

Community Center
The Community Center is on Main Street. It is next to the hospital. It is open from 9 a.m. to 8 p.m. There are English classes in the morning and at night. Call 555-9248 for more information.

MADISON TOWN HALL

Police Station
The police station is on Main Street. Call 911 for emergency help. Call 555-9103 for questions.

Fire Station
The fire station is next to the police station on Main Street. There are two fire trucks.

Madison City Hospital
The hospital is across from the fire station and police station. The emergency room is open 24 hours.

PHONE DIRECTORY

Police Station
555-9103

Fire Station
555-7823

Community Center
555-9248

Hospital
555-6534

POLICE STATION   FIRE STATION

MAIN STREET

COMMUNITY CENTER   HOSPITAL

4 **MATCH** the place to the information.

_____ **1.** police station

_____ **2.** fire station

_____ **3.** community center

_____ **4.** hospital

a. It's next to the police station.

b. It's across from the fire station.

c. The phone number is 555-9103.

d. There are English classes.

Read a brochure. • Write using details.

Writing

1 **WRITE** the name of a store or other place in your city.

Name of place: _____

2 **WRITE** notes about the place.

Street: _____

Location: _____

Hours: _____

There is/are _____.

3 **WRITE** about the place in your city.

Welcome to Madison!
There are many government services in Madison.

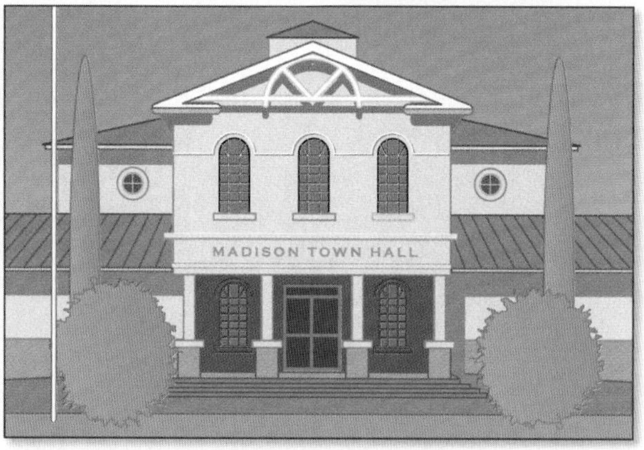

MADISON TOWN HALL

Community Center
The community center is on Main Street. It is next to the hospital. It is open from 9 A.M. to 8 P.M. There are English classes in the morning and at night. Call 555-9248 for more information.

Welcome to _____!
                        (city)

_____
                        (place)

The _____ is _____.

It is _____.

It is open from _____ to _____.

There _____.

1 READ and listen.

Panel 1: Hello. Welcome to the Madison Employment Office. Can I help you?

MADISON EMPLOYMENT OFFICE

PULL

Panel 2: There are two schools near here. One is on the corner of Main Street and 10th Avenue ...

Panel 3: It's five blocks from my apartment.

Panel 4: There are medical classes here!

2 TALK. Answer the questions.

1. Where is the school?

2. What classes are there at the school?

3. How far is the school from Isabel's apartment?

4. How does Isabel feel?

3 WHAT ABOUT YOU? Answer the questions about your school.

1. Where is your school? _____

2. What classes are at your school? _____

3. How far is your school from your apartment or house? _____

Check Your Progress!

Skill	Circle the answer.	Is it correct?
A. Talk about locations.	1. The gas station isn't behind the supermarket. It's **in front of** / **between** the supermarket. 2. The post office is **between** / **next to** the library and the bank. 3. The hospital isn't across from the fire station. It's **next to** / **between** the fire station.	☐ ☐ ☐

		Number Correct	0	1	2	3

Skill	Circle the answer.	Is it correct?
B. Talk about places in the community.	4. There are nurses at the **hospital** / **gas station**. 5. There are cooks at a **library** / **restaurant**. 6. There is a sales clerk at the **supermarket** / **police station**.	☐ ☐ ☐

		Number Correct	0	1	2	3

Skill	Circle the answer.	Is it correct?
C. Use imperatives.	7. **Turn** / **Turns** right on 1st Avenue. 8. She **park** / **parks** next to the supermarket. 9. **Stop** / **Stops** in front of the house.	☐ ☐ ☐

		Number Correct	0	1	2	3

Skill	Circle the answer.	Is it correct?
D. Give directions.	10. Go **straight** / **left** on Elm Street. 11. Don't **stop** / **turn**. It's a one-way street. 12. Do not enter. Make a **U-turn** / **Go straight**.	☐ ☐ ☐

		Number Correct	0	1	2	3

COUNT the number of correct answers above. Fill in the bubbles.

Chart Your Success				
Skill	Need more practice	Okay	Good	Excellent!
A. Talk about locations.	⓪	①	②	③
B. Talk about places in the community.	⓪	①	②	③
C. Use imperatives.	⓪	①	②	③
D. Give directions.	⓪	①	②	③

LESSON 1: Grammar and Vocabulary

1 GRAMMAR PICTURE DICTIONARY. Listen and repeat.

TCD2, 30
SCD, 31

1. She **is buying** a dress.

2. He **is looking** for a book.

3. She **is shopping** with her children.

4. They **are working** at the cash register.

5. The salesclerk **is helping** the customer.

6. The girls **are talking**.

7. She **is trying on** a jacket.

8. They **are carrying** bags.

9. They **are waiting** in line.

2 NOTICE THE GRAMMAR. Look at Activity 1. Underline *is* and *are*. Circle the verbs + *-ing*.

The *present continuous tense* is also called the *present progressive tense*.

Present Continuous

We use the present continuous tense for actions happening now.

Affirmative Statements

Subject	*be*	Verb + *-ing*	noun
I	am		
You	are		
He She	is	buying	pants.
We You They	are		

Negative Statements

Subject	*be* + *not*	Verb + *-ing*	Noun
I	'm not		
You	aren't		
He She	isn't	buying	a jacket.
We You They	aren't		

---

3 **WRITE.** Complete the sentences. Use the present progressive (affirmative or negative).

1. She ___is___ ___buying___ (buy) books.
2. She ___isn't___ ___buying___ (not buy) a backpack.
3. Susana _____ _____ (shop) with her sister.
4. They _____ _____ (not wait) for their friend.
5. I _____ _____ (not talk) to Manuel.
6. Kyung _____ _____ (carry) three bags.
7. We _____ _____ (look for) new backpacks.
8. Ana and Jeff _____ _____ (work) at the supermarket.

4 **WHAT ABOUT YOU?** Look around your classroom. Write a sentence for each verb.

Examples: *Steven is talking to Milena.*

Steven isn't talking to Scott.

1. talk _____
2. write _____
3. listen _____
4. read _____

TALK. Read your sentences to a partner.

LESSON 2: Grammar Practice Plus

1 **WRITE** the colors. Use the words in the box.

| red | orange | yellow | blue | green | purple | white | brown | black |

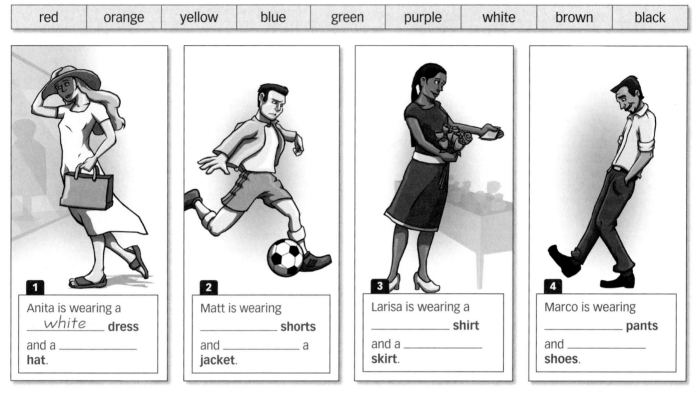

1
Anita is wearing a
_____white_____ **dress**
and a _____
hat.

2
Matt is wearing
_____ **shorts**
and _____ a
jacket.

3
Larisa is wearing a
_____ **shirt**
and a _____
skirt.

4
Marco is wearing
_____ **pants**
and _____
shoes.

TCD2, 31

LISTEN and repeat. Are your answers correct?

2 **WRITE.** What are your classmates wearing? Write three clothing words in the chart.
Then count the number of each color.

Clothing	red	orange	yellow	blue	green	purple	white	brown	black
Example: *shirt*	/		/	///			////		//
1.									
2.									
3.									

3 **GAME.** Write about a person in your class. Don't write the person's name. Read your sentences to three classmates. Your classmates guess the student.

> He's tall. He's wearing blue pants and a red shirt. He's wearing a jacket.

> Is it Ali?

> Yes!

4 TALK about the picture.

Lydia is carrying two bags

WOMEN'S CHANGE   MEN'S CHANGE   Skirts

Brad

SHOES

TCD2, 32

5 LISTEN. Complete the sentences.

1. Brad is wearing red _____*pants*_____ .

2. Marta is wearing a purple _____ .

3. Clara is buying white _____ .

4. Ali is _____ for his wife.

5. Paula is _____ Marta.

6. Oscar is _____ four bags.

6 WRITE. Find the people in the picture. Write their names on the picture.

7 CHECK ☑ the answers.

1. Is Ali waiting in line?   ☐ Yes, he is.   ☐ No, he isn't.

2. Is Oscar helping his brother?   ☐ Yes, he is.   ☐ No, he isn't.

3. Is Clara trying on clothes?   ☐ Yes, she is.   ☐ No, she isn't.

4. Is Marta looking for skirts?   ☐ Yes, she is.   ☐ No, she isn't.

TALK. Ask and answer the questions with a partner.

LESSON 3: Listening and Conversation

1 LISTEN. Circle the correct letter.

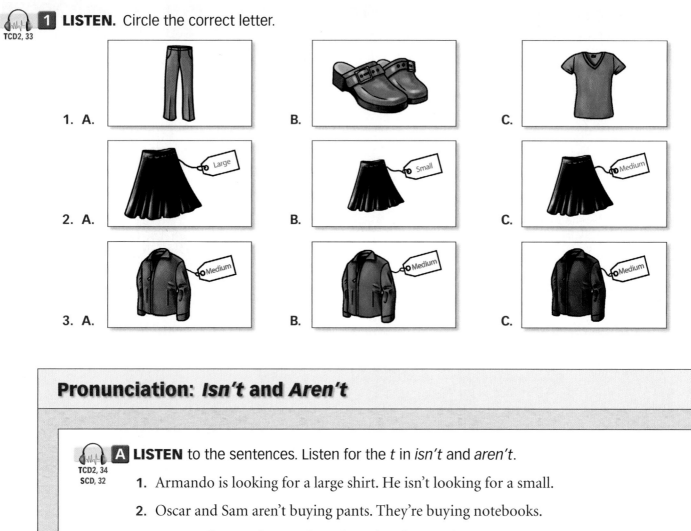

1. A.   B.   C.

2. A. Large   B. Small   C. Medium

3. A. Medium   B. Medium   C. Medium

Pronunciation: *Isn't* and *Aren't*

A LISTEN to the sentences. Listen for the *t* in *isn't* and *aren't*.

TCD2, 34
SCD, 32

1. Armando is looking for a large shirt. He isn't looking for a small.

2. Oscar and Sam aren't buying pants. They're buying notebooks.

3. Lisa is talking to her mother. She isn't talking to her sister.

LISTEN AGAIN and repeat.

B LISTEN to the sentences. Circle *is* or *isn't*, *are* or *aren't*.

TCD2, 35
SCD, 33

1. Oscar **is** / **isn't** buying brown pants.

2. Sara and Maria **are** / **aren't** looking for a black skirt.

3. Mark **is** / **isn't** trying on a blue jacket.

4. They **are** / **aren't** looking for a red shirt.

C TALK. Read the sentences in B to your partner.

TCD2, 36
SCD, 34

2 **LISTEN** and read.

A: Hello. Can I help you?

B: Yes, I'm looking for **pants**.

A: What color?

B: **Black**.

A: And what size?

B: **Medium**.

A: Okay. They're over here.

B: Thank you!

CLOTHING SIZES	
Extra Small	XS
Small	S
Medium	M
Large	L
Extra Large	XL

LISTEN AGAIN and repeat. Then practice with a partner.

3 **PRACTICE THE CONVERSATION** with a partner.

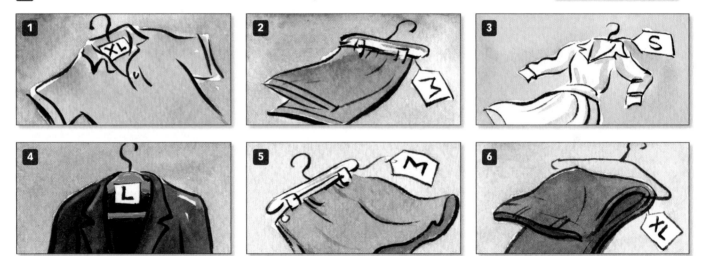

4 **WRITE.** You are shopping for clothes. Make a list of clothes you are looking for. Write the colors and sizes.

You are buying clothes for:	Clothing Item	Color	Size
a job interview			
a New Year's Eve party			
the first day of class			

TALK with a partner. Practice conversations for the clothes on your list. Use the conversation in Activity 2.

LESSON 4: Grammar and Vocabulary

 1 **GRAMMAR PICTURE DICTIONARY.** Listen and repeat.

TCD2, 37
SCD, 35

How much is it?

1 a penny / one cent / 1¢ / $.01

2 a nickel / five cents / 5¢ / $.05

3 a dime / ten cents / 10¢ / $.10

4 a quarter / twenty–five cents / 25¢ / $.25

5 a dollar / $1.00

6 five dollars / $5.00

7 ten dollars / $10.00

8 twenty dollars / $20.00

9
A: How much is the pen?
B: It's **a dollar-fifty**.

10
A: **How much are** the hats?
B: They're **five-forty**.

11
A: **How much are** the sweaters?
B: They're **twenty-two fifty**.

12
A: **How much is** the backpack?
B: It's **fifteen seventy-five**.

2 **NOTICE THE GRAMMAR.** Look at Activity 1. Circle *How much*. Underline *is* and *are*.

Identify U.S. coins and bills. • Use *How much* to ask about prices.

How Much Questions with Be

We ask *How much* to learn the cost of something.

Questions			Answers	
How much	*be*	**Noun**	*It's / They're*	**Noun**
How much	is	the purple dress? the black jacket?	It's	twenty-five dollars. thirty-seven dollars. fifteen dollars.
	are	the blue shoes? the yellow jackets?	They're	

3 **WRITE** the amounts.

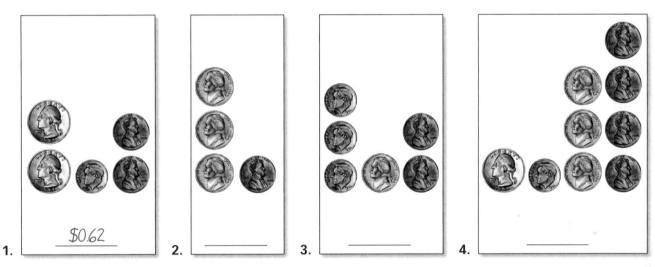

1. $0.62

2. _____

3. _____

4. _____

4 **WRITE.** Complete the questions. Use *is* or *are*. Then answer the questions.

$15.75 $29.99

$24.99

$12.50

1. A: How much ___is___ the green shirt?

   B: _____ It's $15.75. _____

2. A: How much _____ the blue pants?

   B: _____

3. A: How much _____ the white shorts?

   B: _____

4. A: How much _____ the brown hat?

   B: _____

TALK. Practice conversations with a partner.

LESSON 5: Grammar Practice Plus

1 **WRITE.** Complete the sentences. Use the words in the box.

these	that	those	this

1. _____ shirt is seven dollars.

2. _____ skirt is twenty-five dollars.

3. _____ jackets are fifty dollars.

4. _____ hats are thirty-two dollars.

TCD2, 38

LISTEN and repeat. Are your answers correct?

2 **CIRCLE** the correct word.

1. **This /** **These** shirts are $20.00.

2. **That / Those** skirt is $25.00.

3. **This / Those** dress is $35.00.

4. **This / These** jacket is $22.00.

5. **These / That** hats are $8.00.

Math: Money

A **WRITE.** Complete the chart.

1.	25¢		twenty-five cents
2.		$0.84	eighty-four cents

3.		$0.55	fifty-five cents
4.	19¢		nineteen cents

B **WRITE** the words.

1. $5.65   *five dollars and sixty-five cents* _____

2. $2.74   _____

3. $18.12   _____

4. $42.31   _____

Use demonstratives to identify clothing. • Interpret a receipt.

3 TALK with a partner. Student A, look at the picture below. Student B, look at page 198. Point to the pictures and talk with your partner. Write the prices of the clothes.

GAME. Now describe a clothing item to your partner. Your partner guesses the item.

4 LISTEN to the conversations. Correct the prices.

TCD2, 39–41

1

CLOTHES CORNER
1465 Main Street
(415) 555-7943

Item	Price
Shirt	*$7.00* ~~$8.00~~
Dress	$40.00
Hat	$12.00
TOTAL	$60.00

2

CLOTHES CORNER
1465 Main Street
(415) 555-7943

Item	Price
Pants	$32.00
Shirt	$7.00
Skirt	$15.00
TOTAL	$54.00

3

CLOTHES CORNER
1465 Main Street
(415) 555-7943

Item	Price
Shorts	$19.00
Shoes	$40.00
Jacket	$22.00
TOTAL	$81.00

LESSON 6: Apply Your Knowledge

1 **READ** the advertisement. Circle the sale prices.

Clothes Corner Super Labor Day Sale!

Women's Pants — $40 ($29)

Men's Shorts — $25 $19

Dresses — $60 $40

Children's Shirts — $15 $7

Hats — $18 $12

Skirts — $29 $15

Men's Shoes — $49 $35

Jackets — $35 $22

2 **LISTEN** to the radio ad. Circle the clothes you hear about in the ad above.

TCD2, 42

3 **WRITE.** Look at the ad above. Write a shopping list with five things from Clothes Corner for you or a person in your family.

Shopping List

4 LISTEN and read.

TCD2, 43
SCD, 36

A: Hello! Welcome to Clothes Corner! Can I help you?

B: Yes, I'm looking for a **blue dress**. Are **the dresses** on sale?

A: Yes, they are!

B: How much are **these dresses**?

A: They're **$40**.

B: Wow! That's a good price!

LISTEN and repeat. Then practice with a partner.

5 PRACTICE THE CONVERSATION with a partner. Use your shopping list from Activity 3 on page 96.

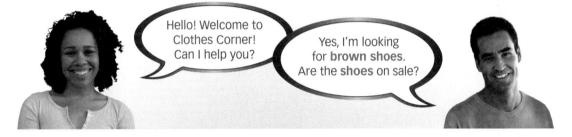

Hello! Welcome to Clothes Corner! Can I help you?

Yes, I'm looking for **brown shoes**. Are the **shoes** on sale?

6 WRITE. Use your shopping list. Write a receipt. Then write a check to Clothes Corner.

CLOTHES CORNER
1465 Main Street
(415) 555-7943

Item	Price
_____	_____
_____	_____
_____	_____
_____	_____
TOTAL	$ _____

Lisa Brown   476
58 Oak Lane
Centerville, New York 13346   Date: _5/29/09_

To _Clothes Corner_____ $ | 59.00 |
Fifty nine with 0/100 ~~~~~~~~ dollars

For _clothes for work_____   _Lisa Brown_
⑈012345⑈ ⑆123456543⑆01234567⑈

                                                              567
                                        Date: _____

To _____ $ [   ]
_____ dollars

For _____ _____
⑈012345⑈ ⑆123456543⑆01234567⑈

7 TALK with a partner about the new clothes you are buying.

LESSON 7: Reading

1 **THINK ABOUT IT.** Where can you buy clothes in your city?

Reading Tip

Look at the words under pictures. They help you learn information.

2 **BEFORE YOU READ.** Look at the sentences under the pictures in the article below. What are the names of the people in the pictures?

3 **READ** the newspaper article. Underline the sentences in quotation marks (" ").

BACK-TO-SCHOOL SALES

It's that time of year again! It's time to go back to school. Young people are looking for fun new clothes. Parents are shopping for good prices. Where are they shopping? What's important to them? Read about these people and find out.

Mary, a mother of three, is shopping today at Clothes Mart. She says, "The service is very good. The sales clerks are friendly and helpful."

Joe is a father of five. He is buying his family's clothes at Value Clothes. "The prices are excellent!" he says.

Tina, 19, is a student. She says, "I 'm looking for my school clothes at COOL Clothes. There's a great selection – there are a lot of good colors and many sizes."

4 **WRITE.** Complete the chart.

	Shopper's Name	Store Name	What is good?
1.	Mary	Clothes Mart	service
2.	Joe		
3.	Tina		

Writing

Writing Tip

Quotes are the words a person says. Quotes make your writing interesting.
Example: "The prices are excellent," he says.

1 WRITE the sentences as quotes.

1. Pedro: I'm shopping at Tall-Mart. The prices are really good!
   Pedro says, "I'm shopping at Tall-Mart. The prices are really good!"
2. Alicia: I'm looking for clothes for school at Low Price Village.
   ____
3. Paul: My friend and I are buying our shoes at Skater's World.
   ____
4. James: I'm at Amazing Apparel. The service is excellent here.
   ____
5. Musa: I'm a nurse. I'm shopping for nurse clothes at Neat Nurses.
   ____

2 WRITE. Look at the article on page 98. Then complete the article below. Tell where each person is shopping: *Clothes Mart, Value Clothes,* or *COOL Clothes*. Write a quote for each person.

WHAT'S IMPORTANT TO YOU?

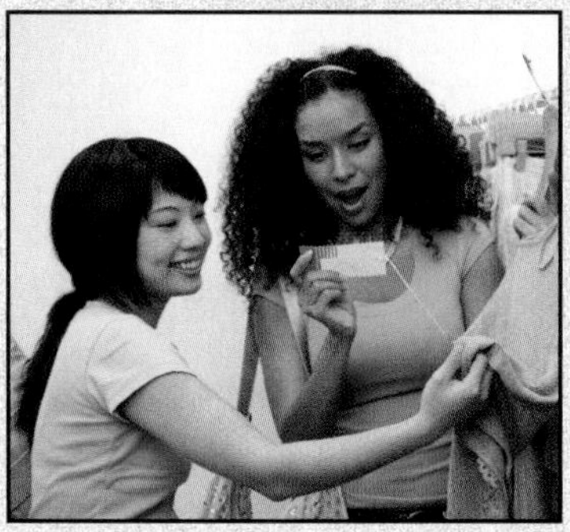

Beth and Cindy are shopping at ______________ Value Clothes.
Beth says, "Wow, that's a good ______________!"

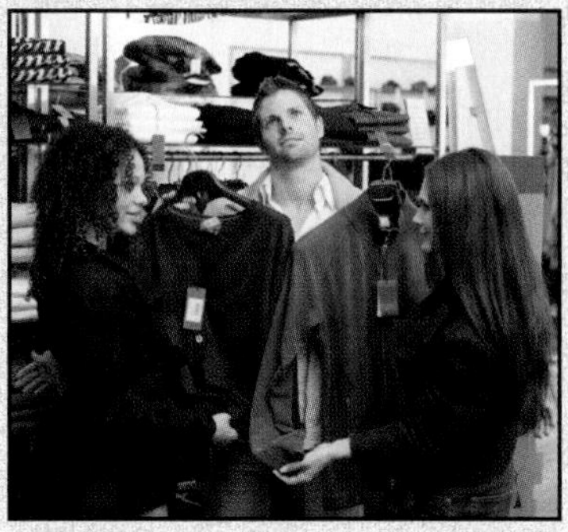

David is ______________ ______________.
____
____
______________.

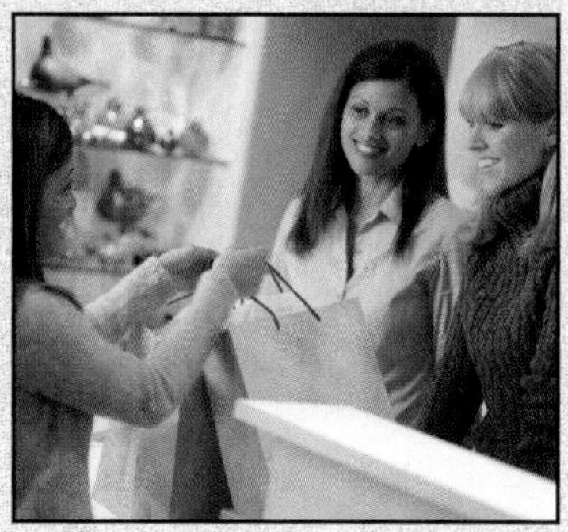

Claudia and Denise ______________ ______________.
____
____
______________.

Career Connection

1 READ and listen.

How much are the classes, Isabel?

One class is $350. The other class is $275. Books are $50 for each class.

How much is your apartment?

$650.

Hmmm… Money is tight. I'll take the $275 class.

2 WRITE. Answer the questions.

1. What is Isabel reading? _____

2. How much is gas for Isabel's car each month? _____

3. How much is food each month? _____

4. How much is Isabel's apartment each month? _____

Expenses:

Gas for car: $75/month

Food: $300/month

Apartment: $650/month

3 WHAT ABOUT YOU? Write a list of your expenses each month.

Check Your Progress!

Skill	Circle the answer.	Is it correct?
A. Use present continuous.	1. Lydia **is waiting** / **are waiting** for her friend. 2. Hector and Ella **are talk** / **are talking**. 3. Paul **is working** / **not is working** at the store.	○ ○ ○

Number Correct | 0 | 1 | 2 | 3

Skill	Circle the answer.	Is it correct?
B. Talk about clothing.	4. Michael is wearing shorts. He's not wearing **pants** / **a shirt**. 5. Elena is wearing a skirt. She's not wearing **a dress** / **a shirt**. 6. Hugo is wearing pants. He's not wearing **a dress** / **a jacket**.	○ ○ ○

Number Correct | 0 | 1 | 2 | 3

Skill	Circle the answer.	Is it correct?
C. Ask about prices.	7. How much **is** / **are** those pants? 8. How much **is** / **are** this shirt? 9. How much **is** / **are** these jackets?	○ ○ ○

Number Correct | 0 | 1 | 2 | 3

Skill	Circle the answer.	Is it correct?
D. Write money amounts.	10. These skirts are **$30.00** / **thirty dollars and no cents**. 11. Those shoes are **$25.95** / **twenty-five and ninety-five dollars**. 12. The hat is **$1299** / **twelve dollars and ninety-five cents**.	○ ○ ○

Number Correct | 0 | 1 | 2 | 3

COUNT the number of correct answers above. Fill in the bubbles.

Chart Your Success				
Skill	Need more practice	Okay	Good	Excellent!
A. Use present continuous.	⓪	①	②	③
B. Talk about clothing.	⓪	①	②	③
C. Ask about prices.	⓪	①	②	③
D. Write money amounts.	⓪	①	②	③

LESSON 1: Grammar and Vocabulary

1 GRAMMAR PICTURE DICTIONARY. Listen and repeat.

TCD2, 45
SCD, 37

1. Jim **gets up** at 7:00.

2. Then he **takes** a shower.

3. He **gets dressed** at 7:15.

4. They **eat** breakfast at 7:45.

5. Jim **brushes** his teeth at 8:30.

6. Abby **does homework** in the afternoon.

7. Jim **cooks** dinner.

8. Karen **reads** books at night.

9. Abby and Amy **go to bed** at 8:00.

2 NOTICE THE GRAMMAR. Look at Activity 1. Circle the verbs that end in *s*. Underline the subjects in these sentences.

Simple Present Tense Statements

The verbs *go* and *do* are irregular with *he/she*.
Thomas goes to class. Julia does her homework.

We use the simple present tense to talk about routines and daily activities.

Affirmative Statements

Subject	Verb
I You	work.
He She	works.
We You They	work.

Negative Statements

Subject	*don't/doesn't*	Verb
I You	don't	work.
He She	doesn't	works.
We You They	don't	work.

3 **CIRCLE** the correct form of the verb.

1. Elena **get up** / **gets up** at 6:30 A.M.

2. Manuel and Jose **doesn't cook** / **don't cook** dinner.

3. Sanjay **doesn't eat** / **don't eat** breakfast with his parents.

4. Claudia **do** / **does** homework in the afternoon.

5. Maya and I **doesn't read** / **don't read** the newspaper in the morning.

4 **WRITE.** Complete the sentences with the correct form of the verb.

1. Eva and Michael _____*read*_____ (read) books at night.

2. Ana _____ (not cook) breakfast with her mother.

3. We _____ (eat) dinner at 8:00.

4. They _____ (not sleep) eight hours at night.

5. Maria _____ (take) a shower in the morning.

5 **WHAT ABOUT YOU?** Talk with a partner.
What do you do _____?

- in the morning
- in the afternoon
- at night

What do you do in the morning?

I go to work.

LESSON 2: Grammar Practice Plus

TCD2, 46

1 LISTEN and repeat.

Adverbs of Frequency

100% ←   → 0%

always	usually	sometimes	never
I **always** get up at 7 A.M.	He **usually** eats breakfast.	They **sometimes** cook dinner.	We **never** get up before 9:00.

2 WRITE. Look at Miguel's schedule. Complete the sentences.

Sunday	Monday	Tuesday	Wednesday	Thursday	Friday	Saturday
7 A.M. eat breakfast	7 A.M. eat breakfast	7 A.M. eat breakfast	7 A.M. eat breakfast	7 A.M. eat breakfast	7 A.M. eat breakfast	7 A.M. eat breakfast
7:30 A.M. read the newspaper	7:30 A.M. read the newspaper	7:30 A.M. read the newspaper	7:30 A.M. read the newspaper	8 A.M.–10 A.M. class	7:30 A.M. read the newspaper	7:30 A.M. read the newspaper
6 P.M. dinner with Steve	9 A.M.–5 P.M. work	9 A.M.–5 P.M. work	2–4 P.M. homework at library	5 P.M. read the newspaper	10 A.M.–12 P.M. work	10 A.M.–3 P.M. work
11 P.M. go to bed	10 P.M. talk to family	8 P.M. dinner with Lara	11 P.M. go to bed	7 P.M. dinner with Pablo and Lisa	1–4 P.M. homework at library	11 P.M. go to bed
	11 P.M. go to bed	11 P.M. go to bed		11 P.M. go to bed	11 P.M. go to bed	

1. Miguel _____always_____ eats breakfast at 7 A.M.

2. He _____ reads the newspaper in the morning.

3. Miguel _____ does his homework at the library.

4. Miguel _____ works.

5. Miguel _____ eats with his friends in the evening.

6. He _____ goes to bed at 11 P.M.

3 WHAT ABOUT YOU? Complete the sentences about you.

1. I _____ get up before 7 A.M.

2. I _____ cook breakfast.

3. I _____ eat dinner with my family.

4. I _____ read at night.

5. I _____ go to bed before 10 P.M.

6. I _____ take a shower at night.

TALK. Read your sentences to a partner.

4 **TALK** about the picture. Describe the family's daily activities.

It's 9:00 in the morning.

5 **LISTEN.** Number the people in the picture.

TCD2, 47

6 **WRITE** sentences about the family's Saturday morning activities.

At 9:00 on Saturday mornings…

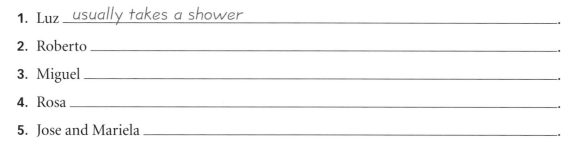

1. Luz _usually takes a shower_____.

2. Roberto _____.

3. Miguel _____.

4. Rosa _____.

5. Jose and Mariela _____.

7 **WHAT ABOUT YOU?** Talk to a partner. What do you do on Saturdays?

LESSON 3: Listening and Conversation

1 **LISTEN.** (Circle) the correct letter.

1. A.   B.   C.

2. A.   B.   C.

3. A.   B.   C.

2 **LISTEN.** Lisa is talking about her schedule. Number the pictures in order.

⬜   ⬜   ⬜   1

LISTEN AGAIN. Match.

1. _____ Lisa gets up at 6:00   **a.** sometimes

2. _____ Lisa cooks dinner   **b.** usually

3. _____ Lisa reads at night   **c.** always

3 **LISTEN** and read.

> A: What are you doing?
>
> B: I'm **eating lunch**.
>
> A: At **11:00 in the morning**?
>
> B: Yes … I usually **eat lunch at 11:00 in the morning**.
>
> A: Really?

LISTEN AGAIN and repeat. Then practice with a partner.

4 **PRACTICE THE CONVERSATION** with a partner.

1 work/9:30 at night

2 take a shower/ 5:00 in the morning

3 talk on the phone/ 11:00 at night

4 cook dinner/ 4:00 in the afternoon

5 eat dinner/10:00 at night

6 go to bed/8:00 in the evening

5 **GAME.** Work in a small group. Say an activity you do and when you do the activity. Listen to your classmates, then say their activities.

I usually do homework at night.

I sometimes sleep in the afternoon.

She usually does homework at night. He sometimes sleeps in the afternoon. I…

LESSON 4: Grammar and Vocabulary

 1 GRAMMAR PICTURE DICTIONARY. Listen and repeat.

TCD2, 51
SCD, 39

1
A: Does he **go to school** at night?
B: Yes, he does.

2
A: Does she **take a class** on Mondays?
B: No, she doesn't.

3
A: Does he **study** in the morning?
B: No, he doesn't.

4
A: Does she **walk to school** with a friend?
B: No, she doesn't.

5
A: Does he **drive to work** every day?
B: Yes, he does.

6
A: Do they **ride the bus**?
B: Yes, they do.

7
A: Does she **call her family** at night?
B: Yes, she does.

8
A: Does he **watch television** at night?
B: Yes, he does.

9
A: Do they **play soccer** on Saturdays?
B: Yes, they do.

2 NOTICE THE GRAMMAR. Read the questions. Circle *Do* or *Does*. Underline the subject.

| Ask and answer *yes/no* questions in the simple present tense.

Yes/No Questions in the Simple Present Tense

Questions			
Do/ Does	**Subject**	**Verb**	
Do	I you		
Does	he she	work	on Tuesdays?
Do	we you they		

Short Answers						
	Subject	**do/ does**			**Subject**	**don't/ doesn't**
	I you	do.			I you	don't.
Yes,	he she	does.	No,		he she	doesn't.
	we you	do.			we you they	don't.

3 **CIRCLE** the correct words.

A: Hi! My name is Mario.

B: Nice to meet you. I'm Lara. **(Do)**/ **Does** you work here?
    ₁

A: Yes, I **do**/ **don't**. I work on Mondays, Wednesdays, and Fridays.
         ₂

B: **Do**/ **Does** you go to school, too?
     ₃

A: Yes, I **do**/ **does**. I go to school on Thursdays.
         ₄

B: Me, too!

4 **WHAT ABOUT YOU?** Put the words in order to make questions. Then check ☑ the right answer for *you*.

1. you/work/on/Do/Mondays?

*Do you work on Mondays?*_____   ☐ Yes, I do.   ☐ No, I don't.

2. play soccer/Do/you/with your friends?

_____   ☐ Yes, I do.   ☐ No, I don't.

3. Does/eat dinner/your family/together?

_____   ☐ Yes, we do.   ☐ No, we don't.

4. the bus?/you/ride/Do

_____   ☐ Yes, I do.   ☐ No, I don't.

TALK with a partner. Ask and answer the questions.

LESSON 5: Grammar Practice Plus

1 **WRITE.** Answer the questions.

1
Does Rosa **arrive** at 9:00 A.M.?
Yes, she does.

2
Does Alicia **take a break** at 12:15 P.M.?
_____

3
Do they **leave** work at 5:00 P.M.?
_____

4
Does she **come home** at 7 P.M.?
_____

 LISTEN and repeat. Are your answers correct?

TCD2, 52

2 **WRITE.** Complete the conversations. Use _do_ or _does_ and the verb.

1. A: _____Does_____ Marie _____work_____ (work) on Mondays?

   B: Yes, she _____.

2. A: _____ Hector and Min _____ (arrive) at 8:30 A.M.?

   B: Yes, they _____.

3. A: _____ Henry _____ (take) a break at work?

   B: No, he _____.

4. A: _____ you _____ (leave) work at 5 P.M. on Wednesdays?

   B: No, I _____.

Pronunciation: _Does he/Does she_

 A **LISTEN** and repeat.

TCD2, 53
SCD, 40

1. Does he take classes on Thursdays?
2. Does she arrive at 7 A.M.?
3. Does she take a break at 1 P.M.?
4. Does he come home at 9 P.M.?

B **LISTEN.** Circle _he_ or _she_.

TCD2, 54
SCD, 41

1. Does **he** /(she) drive a car?
2. Does **he** / **she** go to school?
3. Does **he** / **she** work on Saturdays?
4. Does **he** / **she** ride the bus?

TCD2, 55
SCD, 37

4 **LISTEN.** What time does Kristin do each activity? Write the times in the chart.

Activity	Time
1. arrive at work	*8:00 A.M.*
2. leave work	
3. eat dinner	
4. take a class	

5 **WRITE** the answers.

1. Does Kristin arrive at work at 9:00 A.M.? _No, she doesn't. She arrives at 8 A.M._ .

2. Does Kristin leave work at 4:00 P.M.? _____ .

3. Does Kristin eat dinner at 7:00 P.M.? _____ .

4. Does Kristin take a class at 8:00 P.M.? _____ .

6 **WHAT ABOUT YOU?** Complete the question with a word from the box. Ask six classmates your question. Check ☑ *Yes* or *No*.

Do you
study at night?

No, I don't.

Do you _____ **at night?**		
Classmate's Name	Yes	No
1.	○	○
2.	○	○
3.	○	○
4.	○	○
5.	○	○
6.	○	○

call your family
play soccer
shop
study
work
watch TV
read
use the computer

LESSON 6: Apply Your Knowledge

1 **TALK** with a partner. When do the people work?

When does Tony work?

Tony works **on** Mondays and Fridays **from** 9 A.M. **to** 12 P.M.

We use *from... to...* to talk about time.
I work from 9 A.M. to 5 P.M.

WORK SCHEDULE

	Monday	Tuesday	Wednesday	Thursday	Friday	Saturday
9 A.M.	Tony	Bima	Hong	_____	Tony	_____
10 A.M.						
11 A.M.		Hong	_____			
12 P.M.						
1 P.M.	Bima			John	John	
2 P.M.						
3 P.M.		John	Bima			
4 P.M.						
5 P.M.						

2 **LISTEN** to the conversations. Write the names on the work schedule above.

TCD2, 56

Math: Hourly Wages

An **hourly wage** is the money a person earns each hour.

$$\frac{10}{\text{number of hours}} \times \frac{\$8.00}{\text{hourly wage}} = \frac{\$80.00}{\text{total money in one week}}$$

Look at the work schedule in Activity 1. Complete the chart.

Name	Number of hours		Hourly wage		Total money in one week
Bima		x	$8.00	=	$
Hong		x	$8.00	=	$
John		x	$8.00	=	$

Interpret a work schedule. • Compute hourly wages.

3 **LISTEN** and read.

> *A:* Hi! What's wrong?
>
> *B:* **My mother's birthday dinner** is on **Wednesday night**. I work on **Wednesday nights**.
>
> *A:* What about **Hong**? Could **she** work for you?
>
> *B:* Good idea! Thanks!

LISTEN AGAIN and repeat. Then practice with a partner.

4 **PRACTICE THE CONVERSATION** with a partner.

1
My soccer game/ Friday night/Tony

2
My class party/ Monday night/James

3
New student orientation/Thursday afternoon/Patricia

4
School registration/ Tuesday morning/ Mary

5 **WHAT ABOUT YOU?** Work in a group of three students. You and your classmates work together at a restaurant. Think about your schedule this Saturday. Choose a work time for each student. Write the names next to the work times.

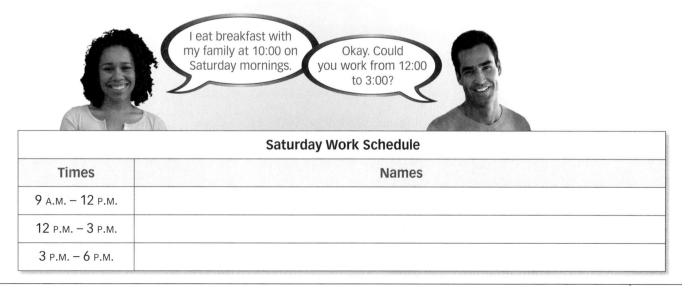

I eat breakfast with my family at 10:00 on Saturday mornings.

Okay. Could you work from 12:00 to 3:00?

Saturday Work Schedule	
Times	**Names**
9 A.M. – 12 P.M.	
12 P.M. – 3 P.M.	
3 P.M. – 6 P.M.	

LESSON 7: Reading

1 **THINK ABOUT IT.** Write words to describe a good father.

_____

_____

2 **BEFORE YOU READ.** Look at the story. Circle three numbers.

3 **READ.** What is the story about? Circle the correct letter.

A. Lorenzo is a teacher.

B. Lorenzo is a good father.

C. Lorenzo has a big family.

Reading Tip

Look for numbers before and after you read. This helps you learn important information.

Busy Man, Good Father

Lorenzo Taylor is a father in Johnsonville. He is a busy man, but he is still a very good father. There are five people in his family: Lorenzo, his wife Lisa, and his three children. Their names are J.R., Tina, and Annie.

Lorenzo is a teacher. He works six days a week at two schools. He gets up early in the morning and arrives at work at six o'clock. He leaves at four o'clock so he can play with his children and help them with their homework. He always spends time with his family at night.

4 **MATCH** the numbers to the information.

___d___ **1.** two   **a.** children

_____ **2.** three   **b.** number of days he works every week

_____ **3.** four   **c.** people in his family

_____ **4.** five   **d.** schools

_____ **5.** six   **e.** time he leaves work

Writing

1 **WRITE** a list of activities you do every day.

Example: _eat breakfast with my children_

_____

_____

_____

_____

_____

2 **WRITE** four activities from your list. Use complete sentences.

Example: First, _I usually get up at 7:00 AM._
Next, _I work from 9 AM. to 4 PM._
Then _I come home at 5:00 PM._
Last, _I go to bed at 10:00 PM._

Writing Tip
Use *first, next, then,* and *last* to put activities in order.

1. First, _____.

2. Next, _____.

3. Then _____.

4. Last, _____.

3 **WRITE** your sentences again on the lines. Use *first, next, then,* and *last*.

Example: _First, I usually get up at 7:15 AM. Next, I work from 9 AM. to 4 PM. Then_
I come home at 5:00 PM. Last, I go to bed at 10:00 PM.

_____

_____

_____

_____

4 **TALK.** Read your sentences to a partner.

Career Connection

1 READ AND LISTEN. Then practice with a partner.

TCD2, 58

1
Are there any good class times, Isabel?

Well, there's a class at 10:15 A.M. on Wednesdays…

2
Do you work on Wednesdays?

Yes, I do.

3
There's also a 10:15 class on Saturday.

Saturday! But we shop on Saturday!

4
Well, I finish work at 5:00 P.M. There's a class on Tuesdays at 6:00 P.M.

Oh good…

2 TALK. Answer the questions.

1. What are Isabel and her friend looking at?

2. Does Isabel work on Wednesdays?

3. Are there classes at night?

4. Does Isabel finish work at 4:00 P.M.?

3 WHAT ABOUT YOU? Isabel talks about three different class times. Are they good or bad class times for you? Talk with a partner.

Example: A: There's a class at _____10:15 AM._____ on _____Wednesdays_____.

B: That's not good for me. I _____work on Wednesdays from 8:00 to 11:00 AM._____.

A: _____That's okay for me_____. I don't work on _____Wednesdays_____.

Check Your Progress!

Skill	Circle the answer.	Is it correct?
A. Use the simple present tense.	1. She **eat** / **eats** breakfast with her family.	☐
	2. Joseph and I **play** / **plays** soccer in the afternoon.	☐
	3. They **clean** / **cleans** the apartment in the morning.	☐

		Number Correct	0	1	2	3

Skill	Circle the answer.	Is it correct?
B. Use adverbs of frequency.	4. Blake is a good student. He **never** / **always** studies.	
	5. Pedro rides the bus six days a week. He **usually** / **sometimes** rides the bus.	☐ ☐ ☐
	6. Ana goes to the library two days a week. She **always** / **sometimes** goes to the library.	

		Number Correct	0	1	2	3

Skill	Circle the answer.	Is it correct?
C. Ask questions with the simple present tense.	7. **Do** / **Does** Roberto and Luz clean on Saturdays?	☐
	8. Does Habiba **take** / **takes** a class?	☐
	9. **Do** / **Does** I work on Saturday?	☐

		Number Correct	0	1	2	3

Skill	Circle the answer.	Is it correct?
D. Talk about daily activities.	10. I don't work on Mondays. I **play soccer** / **drive to my office**.	
	11. I don't go to school on Thursday. I **take a class** / **clean my apartment**.	☐ ☐ ☐
	12. I take a shower in the morning. I don't **brush my teeth** / **cook dinner**.	

		Number Correct	0	1	2	3

COUNT the number of correct answers above. Fill in the bubbles.

Chart Your Success				
Skill	Need more practice	Okay	Good	Excellent!
A. Use the simple present tense.	⓪	①	②	③
B. Use adverbs of frequency.	⓪	①	②	③
C. Ask questions with the simple present tense.	⓪	①	②	③
D. Talk about daily activities.	⓪	①	②	③

LESSON 1: Grammar and Vocabulary

1 **GRAMMAR PICTURE DICTIONARY.** Listen and repeat.

TCD3, 2
SCD, 43

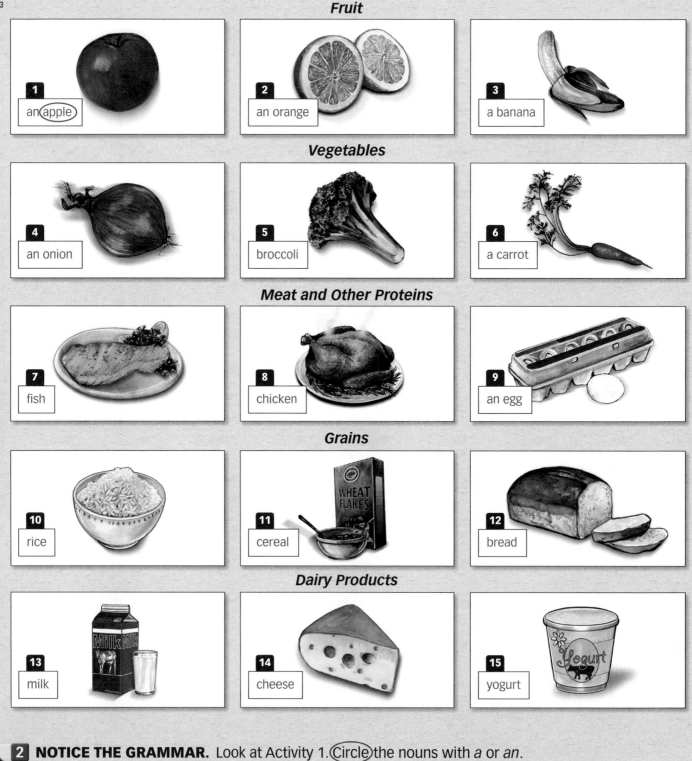

Fruit

1 an apple

2 an orange

3 a banana

Vegetables

4 an onion

5 broccoli

6 a carrot

Meat and Other Proteins

7 fish

8 chicken

9 an egg

Grains

10 rice

11 cereal

12 bread

Dairy Products

13 milk

14 cheese

15 yogurt

2 **NOTICE THE GRAMMAR.** Look at Activity 1. Circle the nouns with *a* or *an*.

Count and Non-count Nouns

Non-count nouns use *is*. *Rice is good.*

We count some nouns (*1, 2, 3 apples*). We don't count other nouns (*milk, water*).

Count Nouns		Non-count Nouns
Article + Singular Noun	**Plural Noun**	
a carrot	carrots	milk
an apple	apples	cheese

3 **WRITE** *C* for count or *N* for non-count.

1. ___C___ apple
2. _____ cereal
3. _____ banana
4. _____ onion

5. _____ broccoli
6. _____ carrot
7. _____ orange
8. _____ yogurt

9. _____ milk
10. _____ rice
11. _____ egg
12. _____ water

4 **CIRCLE** the answer.

1. Milk **is** / **are** a dairy product.
2. Carrots **is** / **are** vegetables.
3. Rice **is** / **are** a grain.

4. Bread **is** / **are** a grain.
5. Broccoli **is** / **are** a vegetable.
6. Oranges **is** / **are** a fruit.

5 **WHAT ABOUT YOU?** Write foods you love, like, and don't like.

	I love 😊😊😊	I like 😊	I don't like 😞
Count			
Non-count Nouns			

TALK to a partner.

I love broccoli.

Really? I don't like broccoli.

LESSON 2: Grammar Practice Plus

1 WRITE the food or drink.

1   a **loaf** of _____bread_____

2   a **carton** of _____

3   a **bag** of _____

4   a **box** of _____

5   a **bottle** of _____

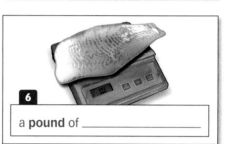

6   a **pound** of _____

LISTEN and repeat. Are your answers correct?

TCD3, 3

2 WRITE. Complete the sentences. Use a word in the box.

bags	~~loaf~~	box	bottle	cartons	pound

1. There's a _____ _loaf_ _____ of bread on the table.

2. I eat a _____ of cereal every week.

3. We usually buy two _____ of rice at the store.

4. A _____ of chicken is only $1.29 today.

5. Tina drinks two _____ of milk every week.

6. Do you want a _____ of juice?

3 WHAT ABOUT YOU? Make a list of foods and drinks you buy.

in a bottle	in a box	in a bag	in a carton	by the pound
juice				

TALK to a partner.

I buy juice in a bottle.

I buy water in a bottle.

4 **TALK** about the picture.

People are shopping for food.

 5 **LISTEN** and write the price.
TCD3, 4

1. _3 pounds/$1.00_   2. _____   3. _____   4. _____

6 **TALK** with a partner. Ask questions about the prices of:

1. a bag of carrots
2. a bottle of orange juice
3. a whole chicken
4. a pound of tuna fish
5. bananas
6. a bag of onions

How much is a bag of carrots?

It's $1.50.

LESSON 3: Listening and Conversation

Pronunciation: Vowel sounds in *eat* and *it*

TCD3, 5
SCD, 44

A **LISTEN** and repeat.

1. fish
2. eat
3. chips

4. cheese
5. it
6. leave

7. live
8. meat
9. sit

TCD3, 6
SCD, 45

B **LISTEN** and circle the word you hear.

1. (live)   leave
2. mitt   meat

3. it   eat
4. chip   cheap

5. sit   seat
6. chick   cheek

C **TALK** with a partner. Say a word in Activity B. Your partner listens and points to the word.

TCD3, 7

1 **LISTEN** and check ☑. What are the people shopping for?

1. ☑ apples   ☐ carrots   ☐ bananas   ☐ oranges
2. ☐ milk   ☐ coffee   ☐ juice   ☐ yogurt
3. ☐ fish   ☐ eggs   ☐ cheese   ☐ chicken
4. ☐ rice   ☐ bread   ☐ cereal   ☐ broccoli

LISTEN AGAIN and complete the chart.

Food	Price	Quantity
1. *apples*		
2.		*a bottle*
3.	$1.29	
4.		

Ask for and give locations in a store. • Interpret a food ad.

2 LISTEN and read.

TCD3, 8
SCD, 46

A: Let's buy some **apples. They're** on sale.

B: How much **are they**?

A: **$1.29 a pound**.

B: Sounds good. Where **are they**?

A: In aisle 5.

LISTEN AGAIN and repeat. Then practice with a partner.

3 PRACTICE THE CONVERSATION with a partner.

Oranges 10/$2.00 (1)	**Chicken** $1.09/pound (2)	**Apple Juice** $1.85/bottle (3)
Bananas $.79/pound (4)	**Bread** $2.35/loaf (5)	**Carrots** $2.50/bag (6)

4 WHAT ABOUT YOU? Walk around the room and talk to your classmates. Complete the chart.

Do you . . .	Classmate's Name
1. buy chicken every week?	
2. like broccoli?	
3. drink juice every morning?	
4. usually eat rice for dinner?	
5. like fish?	

Do you buy chicken every week?

Yes, I do.

LESSON 4: Grammar and Vocabulary

1 GRAMMAR PICTURE DICTIONARY. Listen and repeat.

TCD3, 9
SCD, 47

1
A: What does he usually order for lunch?
B: A **hamburger**.

2
A: What does she usually order for lunch?
B: A **hot dog**.

3
A: What do they usually order for lunch?
B: **Sandwiches**.

4
A: When does she usually eat **salad**?
B: At dinner.

5
A: When does he usually eat **soup**?
B: At lunch.

6
A: When do they usually eat **French fries**?
B: At dinner.

7
A: Where do they usually eat **ice cream**?
B: At the park.

8
A: Where does she usually eat **pie**?
B: At Joe's Bakery.

9
A: Where does he usually drink **soda**?
B: At the movies.

2 NOTICE THE GRAMMAR. Circle *do* or *does*. Underline the verbs.

Information Questions with *Where, When, What*

	Question			Short Answers	
Question Word	***do/does***	**Subject**	**Main Verb**		
Where When What	do	I you	eat?	At Main Street Café.	
	does	he she		At 12:30.	
	do	we you they		Sandwiches and salads.	

---

3 **WRITE.** Complete the sentences with *do* or *does*. Then match.

_*b*_ **1.** What ___*does*___ Tino eat for breakfast?

_____ **2.** When _____ he usually eat dinner?

_____ **3.** Where _____ you buy bread?

_____ **4.** Where _____ Maria shop for food?

_____ **5.** Where _____ Yuri and Olga eat dinner?

_____ **6.** What _____ they usually drink with meals?

a. They usually eat at home.

b. ~~He always eats cereal.~~

c. She shops at GoodMarket.

d. Milk or juice.

e. I usually get it at the bakery.

f. At 6:00.

4 **WHAT ABOUT YOU?** Write your answers.

1. Where do you usually eat lunch? _____ .

2. What do you usually eat for lunch? _____ .

3. When do you usually eat ice cream? _____ .

4. What do you usually eat for breakfast? _____ .

5. Where do you usually buy fruit? _____ .

TALK with a partner. Ask and answer the questions.

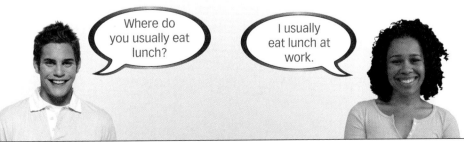

Where do you usually eat lunch?

I usually eat lunch at work.

LESSON 5: Grammar Practice Plus

1 **WRITE.** Complete the sentences with a food or drink.

They **have** _____ *milk* _____.

They **need** _____.

They **want** _____.

TCD3, 10

LISTEN and repeat. Are your answers correct?

2 **WRITE.** Look at the picture. Write the answers.

1. What do they have? _*They have milk.*_____

   _____

   _____

2. What do they need? _____

   _____

   _____

TALK with a partner. Ask and answer the questions above.

3 **WHAT ABOUT YOU?** Complete the chart with foods and drinks.

What do you have in your kitchen?	What do you need at the supermarket?	What do you want at the supermarket?
cereal	*milk*	*ice cream*

TALK with a partner. Ask and answer the questions above.

Use *have, want* and *need.* • Measure food. • Interpret a recipe.

Math: Weights and Measurements

A **READ** the information.

A dozen eggs = 12 eggs   2 pints = 1 quart

3 teaspoons = 1 tablespoon   4 quarts = 1 gallon

2 cups = 1 pint   16 ounces (oz) = 1 pound (lb)

B **WRITE** the amounts.

1. 1/2 dozen eggs = _____ eggs   **4.** 2 gallons = _____ quarts

2. 2 tablespoons = _____ teaspoons **5.** 3 pounds = _____ ounces

3. 10 pints = _____ cups   **6.** 32 ounces = _____ pounds

4 **WRITE.** Look at the recipe for Strata. Write the amounts.

Strata

8 eggs	4 cups milk
1/4 cup butter	1 pound cheese
10 oz. broccoli	1 teaspoon salt
8 pieces of bread	

1. We have a half-dozen eggs. We need ____2____ eggs from the store.

2. There's a pint of milk in the refrigerator. We need _____ more cups.

3. We have 12 ounces of cheese. We need _____ more ounces.

4. We don't have any butter. We need _____ cup.

5. We have 5 ounces of broccoli. We need _____ more ounces.

6. We don't have any bread. We need _____ pieces.

LESSON 6: Apply Your Knowledge

1 **READ** the menu. Answer the questions below.

Main Street Café
1932 Main Street
Tuesday–Sunday • 11 A.M. – 11 P.M.

Sandwiches and Burgers

Chicken Sandwich	$6.95
Tuna Fish Sandwich	$5.95
Egg Salad Sandwich	$4.95
Cheese Sandwich	$4.50
Hamburger	$5.95
Cheeseburger	$6.95
Hot Dog	$4.50

Side Orders

Green Salad		$3.50
Fruit Salad		$3.75
French Fries		$1.95
Potato Chips		$1.00
Soup	cup $1.50	bowl $2.50

Desserts

Ice Cream	$2.00
Apple Pie	$3.00

Beverages

Soda
Iced Tea
Milk
Coffee
Orange Juice
        Large $2.00   Small $3.00

1. What is the name of the restaurant? _____

2. Where is the restaurant? _____

3. When does the restaurant open? _____

4. How many sandwiches are on the menu? _____

2 **LISTEN.** Look at the menu. Circle the foods the woman orders.

TCD3, 11

3 **WRITE.** How much is the woman's lunch?

Sandwich or Burger		$5.95
Side Order	+	
Dessert	+	
Beverage	+	
Total	=	

4 **LISTEN** and read.

TCD3, 12
SCD, 48

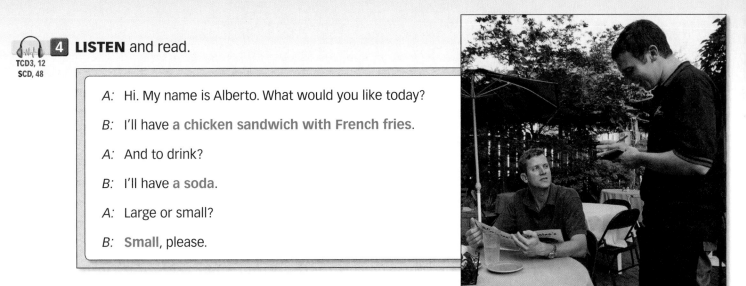

A: Hi. My name is Alberto. What would you like today?

B: I'll have **a chicken sandwich with French fries**.

A: And to drink?

B: I'll have **a soda**.

A: Large or small?

B: **Small**, please.

LISTEN AGAIN and repeat. Then practice with a partner.

5 **PRACTICE THE CONVERSATION** with a partner.

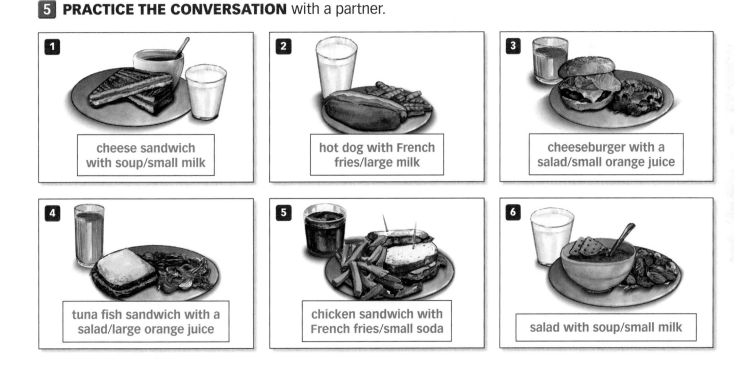

1. cheese sandwich with soup/small milk
2. hot dog with French fries/large milk
3. cheeseburger with a salad/small orange juice
4. tuna fish sandwich with a salad/large orange juice
5. chicken sandwich with French fries/small soda
6. salad with soup/small milk

6 **TALK** with a partner. Order meals from the menu on page 128. Write the things your partner orders.

Sandwiches/Burgers	Side Orders	Desserts	Beverages

LESSON 7: Reading

1 **THINK ABOUT IT.** What do you usually eat for breakfast?

2 **BEFORE YOU READ.** Look at the article. (Circle) the countries.

Reading Tip
Notice connecting words (*and, but*). Which word connects similar ideas? Which word connects different ideas?

3 **READ.** What is the article about? Check ☑ the answer.

☐ Breakfast is healthy.   ☐ Breakfast is different in different countries.

Breakfast Around the World

Most people eat breakfast. People in different countries eat different kinds of food for breakfast. For example, people in Vietnam and China often eat rice and soup for breakfast. In India, people like rice, eggs, and vegetables for breakfast, but people in South America usually eat something small, such as a piece of bread. In the United States and England, people often eat cereal with milk, but people in Russia sometimes eat cereal with cheese. People all over the world drink tea or coffee for breakfast. People in Asia drink tea for breakfast, but in the U.S. and Europe people usually drink coffee.

4 **CHECK** ☑ *similar* or *different*.

	similar	different
1. breakfast food in China and breakfast food in Vietnam		
2. breakfast food in India and breakfast food in South America		
3. breakfast drink in Asia and breakfast drink in Europe		
4. breakfast food in England and breakfast food in the U.S.		
5. breakfast food in Vietnam and breakfast food in the U.S.		

Writing

1 **WRITE.** Look at the diagram. Complete the sentences with *and* or *but*.

For breakfast,

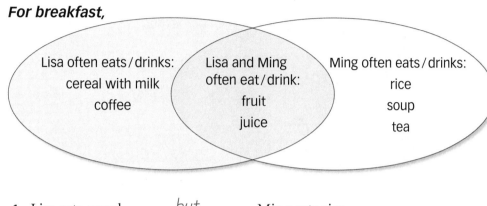

Lisa often eats / drinks:
cereal with milk
coffee

Lisa and Ming
often eat / drink:
fruit
juice

Ming often eats / drinks:
rice
soup
tea

Writing Tip

Use *and* to connect sentences with similar ideas.

Use *but* to connect sentences with different ideas.

1. Lisa eats cereal, _____*but*_____ Ming eats rice.

2. Lisa drinks juice, _____ Ming drinks juice, too.

3. Lisa drinks coffee, _____ Ming drinks tea.

4. Lisa eats fruit, _____ Ming eats fruit, too.

2 **TALK** to a partner about what you eat and drink for breakfast. Complete the diagram.

For breakfast,

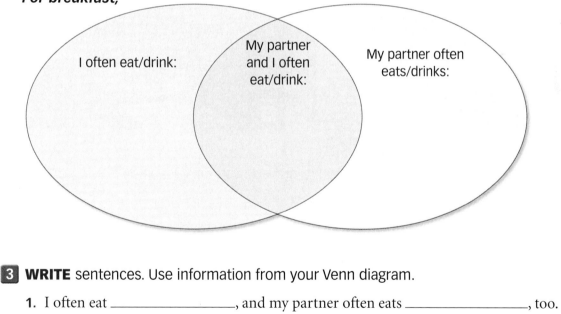

I often eat/drink:

My partner
and I often
eat/drink:

My partner often
eats/drinks:

3 **WRITE** sentences. Use information from your Venn diagram.

1. I often eat _____, and my partner often eats _____, too.

2. I often eat _____, but my partner often eats _____.

3. _____.

4. _____.

5. _____.

1 READ AND LISTEN. Then practice with a partner.

TCD3, 13

2 WRITE. Work with a partner. How much food or drink do you think Isabel needs to get? Complete the chart.

Food/Drinks	How much/How many?
cookies	4 dozen

3 WHAT ABOUT YOU? What food and drinks do you like for a snack?

Check Your Progress!

Skill	Circle the answer.	Is it correct?
A. Use count and non-count nouns.	1. Would you like a **carrot** / **cheese**?	☐
	2. I need **oranges** / **onion** from the store.	☐
	3. **Cheese** / **Bananas** are good for you.	☐

	Number Correct	0	1	2	3

Skill	Circle the answer.	Is it correct?
B. Use information questions with *where, when,* and *what*.	4. What **do** / **does** you want for dinner?	☐
	5. Where does Maria **want** / **wants** to eat?	☐
	6. When **do** / **does** they eat breakfast.	☐

	Number Correct	0	1	2	3

Skill	Circle the answer.	Is it correct?
C. Talk about food.	7. I like ice cream for **salad** / **dessert**.	☐
	8. Do you drink **coffee** / **fish** in the morning?	☐
	9. We need **chicken** / **eggs** for breakfast.	☐

	Number Correct	0	1	2	3

Skill	Circle the answer.	Is it correct?
D. Use quantity words.	10. She buys **a bottle** / **a bag** of soda every day.	☐
	11. He needs **a loaf** / **a pound** of fish.	☐
	12. Do you want **a pound** / **a carton** of juice.	☐

	Number Correct	0	1	2	3

COUNT the number of correct answers above. Fill in the bubbles.

Chart Your Success				
Skill	Need more practice	Okay	Good	Excellent!
A. Use count and non-count nouns.	⓪	①	②	③
B. Use information questions with *where, when,* and *what*.	⓪	①	②	③
C. Talk about food.	⓪	①	②	③
D. Use quantity words.	⓪	①	②	③

LESSON 1: Grammar and Vocabulary

1 GRAMMAR PICTURE DICTIONARY. Listen and repeat.

1 Ming can <u>take</u> patient information.

2 She can **take blood pressure**.

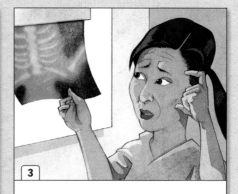

3 She can't **read an x-ray**.

4 Radek can **measure things**.

5 He can **supervise workers**.

6 He can't **drive a forklift**.

7 Bernice can **speak** French.

Bonjour

8 She can **use a scanner**.

9 She can't **fix a copier**.

2 NOTICE THE GRAMMAR. Look at Activity 1. Underline *can* or *can't*. Circle the verbs.

Can for Ability

Can't is short for cannot. We usually say can't.

We use *can* to talk about ability.

Affirmative/Negative Statements

Subject	can/can't	Verb	
I You He She We You They	can can't	drive use speak	a taxi. a copier. English.

Questions

Can	Subject	Verb
Can	I you he she we you they	drive? read?

Answers

Yes/No	Subject	can/can't
Yes,	I you he she we you they	can.
No,		can't.

3 **MATCH.**

_____C_____ **1.** Jim can check teeth.

_____ **2.** Tony can drive a forklift.

_____ **3.** Maya and Seth can drive a taxi.

_____ **4.** Hector can supervise people.

_____ **5.** They can take blood pressure.

_____ **6.** She can use a computer.

a. They are taxi drivers.

b. He is a construction worker.

c. ~~He is a dentist.~~

d. She is an office assistant.

e. He is a supervisor.

f. They are nursing assistants.

4 **WHAT ABOUT YOU?** Check ☑ your answer.

1. Can you drive a car? ☐ Yes, I can. ☐ No, I can't.

2. Can you cook Chinese food? ☐ Yes, I can. ☐ No, I can't.

3. Can you speak three languages? ☐ Yes, I can. ☐ No, I can't.

4. Can you use a copier? ☐ Yes, I can. ☐ No, I can't.

5. Can you fix a car? ☐ Yes, I can. ☐ No, I can't.

6. Can you use a scanner? ☐ Yes, I can. ☐ No, I can't.

TALK with a partner. Ask and answer the questions.

LESSON 2: Grammar Practice Plus

1 MATCH. Complete the sentences. Use the words below.

1

A **plumber** can fix
_____toilets_____.

2

An **accountant** can
use _____.

3

A **electrician** can fix
_____.

4

A **mechanic** can fix
_____.

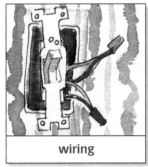

wiring

a calculator

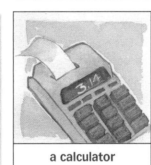

toilets

trucks

TCD3, 15

LISTEN and repeat. Are your answers correct?

2 WRITE. Complete the chart.

Occupations (People)		Tools and Equipment (Things)
A plumber	can fix	*toilets*
	can prepare	
	can use	
	can drive	

3 WHAT ABOUT YOU? Write three things you can do and three things you can't do.

1. I can _____

2. I can _____

3. I can _____

1. I can _____

2. I can _____

3. I can _____

TALK. Read your sentences to a partner.

4 **TALK** about the picture.

Maria is reading an x-ray.

Abdul

Maria

Tim   Henry

EMERGENCY

AMBULANCE

5 **LISTEN.** Complete the sentences. Use *can* or *can't*.

1. Kathy and Jake _____ make lunch.

2. Andy _____ lift the box.

3. Ana _____ fix water pipes.

4. Trung _____ take blood pressure.

5. Greg _____ fix the car.

6. Yuri _____ drive an ambulance.

6 **LOOK** at the sentences above. Write the peoples' names on the picture.

7 **TALK** to a partner. Ask and answer questions.

Can Ana fix water pipes?

Yes, she can.

LESSON 3: Listening and Conversation

 1 **LISTEN** and circle the correct letter.
TCD3, 17

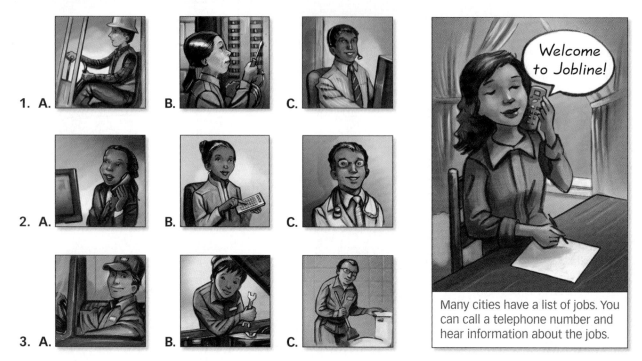

1. A. B. C.

2. A. B. C.

3. A. B. C.

> Welcome to Jobline!
>
> Many cities have a list of jobs. You can call a telephone number and hear information about the jobs.

LISTEN AGAIN. Write the letter on the line for the skill you hear.

1. _____   **a.** fix cars and trucks

2. _____   **b.** speak English and Spanish

3. _____   **c.** use a computer

Pronunciation: *Can* and *Can't*

 A **LISTEN** and circle the letter of the sentence you hear.
TCD3, 18
SCD, 50

1. **A.** I can cook Japanese food.   **B.** I can't cook Japanese food.

2. **A.** She can fix the toilet.   **B.** She can't fix the toilet.

3. **A.** You can drive a bus.   **B.** You can't drive a bus.

B **TALK** with a partner. Read the sentences above.

TCD3, 19
SCD, 51

2 **LISTEN** and read.

> *A:* I want a job as a **construction foreman**.
>
> *B:* Oh. Do you have any skills?
>
> *A:* Yes, I can **supervise workers**.
>
> *B:* That's good. Can you **drive a forklift**?
>
> *A:* No, I can't.

LISTEN AGAIN and repeat. Then practice with a partner.

3 **PRACTICE THE CONVERSATION** with a partner.

1	2	3
accountant/use a calculator/speak Spanish	chef/cook Chinese food/ cook Japanese food	teacher/teach computer skills/speak two languages
4	5	6
nursing assistant/take patient information/read x-rays	office assistant/use a computer/use a scanner	server/serve food/ work until 1 a.m.

 4 **WHAT ABOUT YOU?** Walk around the room and talk to your classmates. Complete the chart.

Can you . . .	Classmate's Name
1. fix electrical problems?	
2. use a computer?	
3. use a calculator?	
4. use a cash register?	

Can you fix electrical problems?

No, I can't.

LESSON 4: Grammar and Vocabulary

1 **GRAMMAR PICTURE DICTIONARY.** Listen and repeat.

We opened our new store today!

My husband **studied** business for four years.

We **borrowed** money from the bank in March.

Painters **painted** our store last month.

We **ordered** the clothing two weeks ago.

We **cleaned the store** last week.

They **delivered the clothes** yesterday.

I **organized the shelves** last night.

We **opened** for business this morning at 9 A.M.

We closed at 8 P.M. and I **counted** our money!

2 **NOTICE THE GRAMMAR.** Look at Activity 1. Underline the verbs. Circle the time expressions (examples: *yesterday*, *last week*).

Past Tense Statements with Regular Verbs

We often use time expressions with the past tense.

Affirmative Statements

Subject	Verb	Time Expression
I You He She We You They	work**ed** stud**ied** mov**ed**	last week. yesterday. last night. in 1999.

Negative Statements

Subject	*didn't*	Verb	Time Expression
I You He She We You They	didn't	work study move	last week. yesterday. last night. in 1999.

3 WRITE. Complete the sentences with the past tense form of the verb.

1. He _____delivered_____ (deliver) your package yesterday.

2. You _____ (study) in the library last Saturday.

3. We _____ (order) supplies last month.

4. I _____ (clean) my apartment last weekend.

5. You _____ (use) the copier yesterday.

6. They _____ (paint) the classroom yesterday.

7. Mark _____ (borrow) my pencil.

8. Lisa _____ (count) the books. We need two more.

4 WHAT ABOUT YOU? Write three things you did and three things you didn't do last night.

Things I did last night:	Things I didn't do:
Example: *I watched TV.*	*I didn't study for a test.*
1.	1.
2.	2.
3.	3.

TALK. Read your sentences to a partner.

I watched TV last night. I didn't study for a test.

LESSON 5: Grammar Practice Plus

1 **LISTEN AND REPEAT.** Then circle the *irregular* past tense verbs.

TCD3, 21

Irregular Past Tense Verbs	
Base Form	**Past Tense Form**
break	broke
go	went
make	made

1 Last week, I **received** a letter from my girlfriend.

2 Yesterday, I (went) to the airport.

3 She **arrived** at 4 P.M.

4 I **made** a nice dinner for her last night.

5 I **washed** the dishes after dinner.

6 Then she **broke** my heart.

2 **WRITE** the past tense form of the verb.

Yesterday, I _____ (work) for 12 hours in our new store. More than 200
 1

customers _____ (visit) the store. One salesclerk _____ (not/come) to
 2 3

work. We _____ (ask) our friend Jung to help. Jung _____ (answer) the
 4 5

telephone and we _____ (help) customers. We _____ (close) the store
 6 7

at 8:00 and _____ (clean) until 9:00. Then we _____ (go) home. It was
 8 9

a busy day, but we _____ (make) a lot of money!
 10

Make statements with irregular past tense verbs. • Interpret a pay stub.

Math: Pay Stubs

Read Ken's pay stub for last week. Match.

Employee name: Ken Trang		Pay Begin Date: 07/24/08	Pay End Date: 07/31/08
Pay Rate	**Hours**	**Current Earnings**	**Year to Date Earnings**
$15.00/hour	40	$600.00	$18,900.00

1. Last week, Ken worked __c__.
2. Last week, he earned _____ an hour.
3. Last week, he earned _____.
4. From 1/1 to 7/31, he earned _____.

a. $600.00
b. $18,900.00
c. ~~40 hours~~
d. $15.00

3 **WHAT ABOUT YOU?** Complete the sentences. Use the affirmative or negative past tense of the verb.

1. I ___*didn't arrive*___ (arrive) at school early today.
2. I _____ (study) yesterday.
3. I _____ (work) 40 hours last week.
4. I _____ (clean) my house yesterday.
5. I _____ (wash) my car last weekend.
6. I _____ (make) dinner last night.
7. I _____ (go) to the supermarket last week.
8. I _____ (receive) an email message yesterday.

TALK. Read your sentences to a partner.

LESSON 6: Apply Your Knowledge

1 READ the job ads. Circle the abbreviations (*FT, PT, M-W, exp.*).

Electrician's Assistants Needed

$12/hour, benefits, Need exp. Fix wiring and other electrical problems.

Call (415) 555-9012

Restaurant Managers Café Henri

Supervise servers, schedule workers, order food. PT. Apply in person at 115 North Main St.

Cooks Café Henri

Make salads and soups. FT. Apply in person at 115 North Main St.

Office Assistant

Can you use a computer and a copier? Do you answer phones? Busy office needs assistant M-W.

Call (415) 555-6600.

---

2 WRITE the word next to the abbreviation.

1. FT ____*full-time*____

2. PT _____

3. M-W _____

4. exp . _____

experience

full-time (35 or more hours per week)

Monday through Wednesday

part-time (less than 40 hours a week)

3 WRITE. Look at the job ads again. Complete the chart.

Position	Skills	How to apply
Electrician's Assistant	*fix wiring, fix other electrical problems*	*Call (415) 555-9012.*
Restaurant Manager		
Cook		
Office Assistant		

4 LISTEN. What job from Activity 1 is good for each person? Complete the chart.

TCD3, 22

Person	Job
#1	*restaurant manager*
#2	
#3	
#4	

Understand job ads. • Interview for a job.

5 **LISTEN** and read.

TCD3, 23
SCD, 53

A: What was your job before?

B: I was an **office assistant**.

A: I see. What did you do?

B: I **answered the telephone and ordered supplies**.

LISTEN AGAIN and repeat. Then practice with a partner.

6 **PRACTICE THE CONVERSATION** with a partner. Use the past tense.

1. accountant/prepare taxes
2. server/serve food
3. cook/cook all kinds of food
4. salesclerk/open the store and help customers
5. nurse/help the doctor
6. construction foreman/ supervise workers

7 **WHAT ABOUT YOU?** Talk with a partner. Ask and answer questions about skills and jobs.

What was your job before?

I was a salesclerk.

What did you do?

I helped customers.

LESSON 7: Reading

1 **THINK ABOUT IT.** What can you do to find a job?

2 **BEFORE YOU READ.** Look at the application. Match the heading to the definition.

Heading	Definition
_____ **1.** Work experience	**a.** things you can do
_____ **2.** Position wanted	**b.** job you want
_____ **3.** Skills	**c.** things you did before

Reading Tip

Use headings to find information on a form.

3 **READ** the application. Answer the questions below.

Job Application								
Name: Sonia Ramirez		**Position wanted:** office manager						
Address: 1913 South Pine Street Oakton, IL 60662		**Hours available:**						
		S	M	T	W	TH	F	S
Telephone Number: (708) 555-6729			8-5	8-5	8-5	8-5	8-5	

Skills: can use a computer, can use a scanner, good people skills, can speak Spanish and English

WORK EXPERIENCE

Present or last position: office assistant

Employer: Oakton Dental Group

Responsibilities: I ordered office supplies, answered the phone, and made copies.

1. What kind of job does Sonia want? _office manager_____

2. What days can Sonia work? _____

3. What hours can Sonia work each day? _____

4. What are her skills? _____

_____

5. Where did Sonia work before? _____

6. What did Sonia do there? _____

_____

Writing

1 **WRITE.** Answer the questions.

1. What kind of job do you want? _____

2. What days can you work each week? _____

3. What hours can you work? _____

4. What are your skills? _____

5. Where did you work before? _____

6. What did you do at your last job? _____

2 **WRITE.** Complete the job application.

Name:	Position wanted:						
Address:	**Hours available:**						
	S	M	T	W	TH	F	S
Telephone Number:							
Skills:							

WORK EXPERIENCE
Present or last position:
Employer:
Responsibilities:

3 **EDIT** your application.

1. ☐ Did you answer all the questions?

2. ☐ Did you write your zip code in your address?

3. ☐ Did you write the area code for your telephone number?

4. ☐ Did you use the correct tense?

5. ☐ Did you spell the words correctly?

Writing Tip

Always edit job applications and other important forms.

Career Connection

1 **READ** and listen. Then practice with a partner.

Great job, Isabel. You worked hard, learned the new computer system…

1

Thank you. Is there anything I need to improve?

2

Well, you sometimes didn't check your spelling in emails.

3

I'm sorry. I'm working on that.

4

2 **WRITE.** Complete the chart.

Things Isabel did well	Things Isabel needs to improve
Learned the new computer system	

3 **WHAT ABOUT YOU?** Talk with a partner. Ask and answer the questions.

1. What did you do well at a past job (or school)?

2. What do you need to improve now?

Set employment goals.

Check Your Progress!

Skill	Circle the answer.	Is it correct?
A. Use *can* for ability.	1. I can **fix** / **fixed** cars. 2. He can **uses** / **use** a computer. 3. She **cans take** / **can take** blood pressure.	☐ ☐ ☐

		Number Correct	0	1	2	3

Skill	Circle the answer.	Is it correct?
B. Use simple past.	4. We **study** / **studied** for a test yesterday. 5. They **didn't** / **don't** work last year. 6. You **worked** / **not worked** last night.	☐ ☐ ☐

		Number Correct	0	1	2	3

Skill	Circle the answer.	Is it correct?
C. Talk about skills and occupations.	7. She's a mechanic. She fixes **cars** / **toilets**. 8. I can fix wiring. I am **a plumber** / **an electrician**. 9. He's **an accountant** / **a cook**. He prepares taxes.	☐ ☐ ☐

		Number Correct	0	1	2	3

Skill	Circle the answer.	Is it correct?
D. Talk about actions at work.	10. Yesterday, I **ordered** / **painted** a house. 11. We **watched** / **cleaned** the store last night. 12. Hong **used** / **cleaned** a scanner in her job as an office assistant.	☐ ☐ ☐

		Number Correct	0	1	2	3

COUNT the number of correct answers above. Fill in the bubbles.

Chart Your Success				
Skill	Need more practice	Okay	Good	Excellent!
A. Use *can* for ability.	⓪	①	②	③
B. Use simple past.	⓪	①	②	③
C. Talk about skills and occupations.	⓪	①	②	③
D. Talk about actions at work.	⓪	①	②	③

LESSON 1: Grammar and Vocabulary

TCD3, 25
SCD, 54

1 GRAMMAR PICTURE DICTIONARY. Listen and repeat.

Last night at 8 o'clock:

1. I was on an **airplane**.
2. Roger was on a **train**.
3. Anna was on a **bus**.
4. Don was at the **airport**.
5. Mia was at the **train station**.
6. Helen was at the **bus stop**.
7. Jack and Tim were at the **baggage claim**.
8. Hector and Rosa were on the **platform**.
9. Paula was at the **ticket counter**.

2 NOTICE THE GRAMMAR. Look at Activity 1. Underline *was* and *were*.

The Simple Past Tense of *Be*

Was and *were* are the past tense of *be*.

	Affirmative			Negative			Contractions
Subject	***was/ were***		**Subject**	***was/were + not***			

Affirmative

Subject	*was/were*	
I	was	happy.
You	were	
He / She / It	was	on the platform.
We / You / They	were	in Mexico in 1999.

Negative

Subject	*was/were + not*	
I	was not	sad.
You	were not	
He / She / It	was not	on the bus.
We / You / They	were not	here.

Contractions

was not = wasn't
were not = weren't

---

3 **CIRCLE** *was* or *were*.

1. I **was** / **were** at the airport at 10:00 last night.

2. You **was** / **were** in Mexico last year.

3. We **was** / **were** on the bus this morning.

4. The trains **was** / **were** in the station.

5. Maria **was** / **were** at the bus stop yesterday at 4 P.M.

6. It **was** / **were** cold yesterday.

7. You **was** / **were** funny at the meeting today.

 4 **WHAT ABOUT YOU?** Complete the sentences. Use *was*.

1. Yesterday afternoon at 3:00, I _____.

2. Yesterday evening at 6:00, I _____.

3. Last night at 8:00, I _____.

4. This morning at 8:00, I _____.

TALK. Read your sentences to a partner.

Yesterday afternoon at 3:00, I was at home.

LESSON 2: Grammar Practice Plus

1 **WRITE.** Complete the sentences with *was* or *were*.

1 Class 9:00–12:00

Three students ___were___ **early** yesterday.

2 Class 9:00–12:00

Four students _____ **on time** yesterday.

3

One student _____ **late**.

4

The classroom _____ **crowded** at 11:00.

5

The classroom _____ **empty** last night.

6

The students _____ **noisy** yesterday.

7

The teacher _____ **quiet** this morning.

LISTEN and repeat. Are your answers correct?

TCD3, 26

2 **WRITE** sentences. Use the negative form of the verb.

1. The bus was messy.   *It wasn't neat.*

2. The train was crowded.   _____

3. The women were quiet.   _____

4. The taxi was on time.   _____

5. The children were noisy. _____

3 **WHAT ABOUT YOU?** Circle the correct word(s).

1. My home was **noisy / quiet** at 8:00 last night.

2. I was **on time / late / early** for class today.

3. Our teacher was **on time / late / early** for class today.

4. Our classroom is **crowded / not crowded** today.

4 **TALK** about the pictures.

5 **LISTEN.** Circle *True* or *False*.

TCD3, 27

1. True (False)   **2.** True   False   **3.** True   False   **4.** True   False

6 **WRITE** sentences about the pictures. Use *was, wasn't, were,* or *weren't*.

1. the airplane/quiet _The airplane wasn't quiet._____

2. it (the weather)/rainy _____

3. the children/noisy _____

4. the baggage claim area and train/crowded _____

7 **TALK.** Think about Paul's trip.
What happened next? Tell a partner.

LESSON 3: Listening and Conversation

 1 **LISTEN** to the phone message. Circle the problem.
TCD3, 28

A. The bus was late.   **B.** Liza was sick.   **C.** The bus was crowded.

LISTEN AGAIN. Look at the bus schedule.
Answer the questions.

	Departs Orlando	Arrives Miami	Travel Time	Fare
A	11:00	5:30	6 hr 30 min	$44.50
B	1:45	7:45	6 hr	$44.50
C	3:15	9:20	6 hr 5 min	$44.50

1. Is Liza on Bus A, B, or C? _____

2. How much is the fare (ticket price)? _____

3. How long is Liza's bus ride? _____

4. When does Liza's bus arrive in Miami? _____

Pronunciation: Interjections

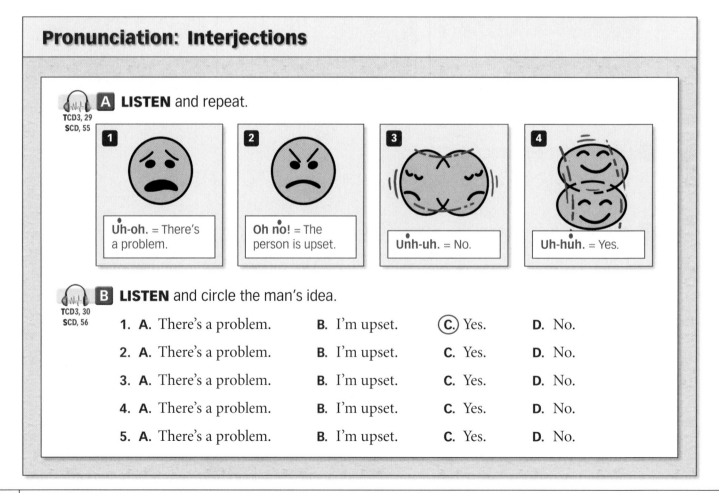

A **LISTEN** and repeat.
TCD3, 29
SCD, 55

1 Uh-oh. = There's a problem.

2 Oh no! = The person is upset.

3 Unh-uh. = No.

4 Uh-huh. = Yes.

B **LISTEN** and circle the man's idea.
TCD3, 30
SCD, 56

1. **A.** There's a problem.   **B.** I'm upset.   **C.** Yes.   **D.** No.

2. **A.** There's a problem.   **B.** I'm upset.   **C.** Yes.   **D.** No.

3. **A.** There's a problem.   **B.** I'm upset.   **C.** Yes.   **D.** No.

4. **A.** There's a problem.   **B.** I'm upset.   **C.** Yes.   **D.** No.

5. **A.** There's a problem.   **B.** I'm upset.   **C.** Yes.   **D.** No.

Interpret a bus schedule. • Apologize for being late.

2 **LISTEN** and read.

TCD3, 31
SCD, 57

> A: I'm sorry I'm late. **The traffic was really bad.**
>
> B: You missed **a meeting**.
>
> A: Oh, no. I'm so sorry.
>
> B: Well, please call next time.

LISTEN AGAIN and repeat. Then practice with a partner.

3 **PRACTICE THE CONVERSATION** with a partner.

1

The train was late/
an important phone call

2

The bus was late/
a delivery

3

The train was too crowded/
a pickup

4

My car broke down/
a delivery

5

My daughter was sick/
an important phone call

6

I missed the bus/
an important customer

4 **WHAT ABOUT YOU?** Walk around the room and talk to your classmates. Complete the chart.

Were you . . .	Classmate's Name
1. early to class today?	
2. late to work last week?	
3. on a bus at 8:00 last night?	
4. in an airport last month?	
5. at home on Saturday at 11 A.M.?	

> Were you early
> to class today?

> Yes, I was.

LESSON 4: Grammar and Vocabulary

 1 **GRAMMAR PICTURE DICTIONARY.** Listen and repeat.

TCD3, 32
SCD, 58

What did you do last weekend?

1

A: I went to the **beach**.
B: Was it **relaxing**?
A: No it wasn't. It was **stressful**.

2

A: I went to a **movie**.
B: Was it **good**?
A: Yes, it was. It was **exciting**!

3

A: I went to a **museum**.
B: Was it **interesting**?
A: No it wasn't. It was **boring**.

4

A: I went to **an amusement park**.
B: Was it **fun**?
A: Yes, it was. It was **scary**, too!

2 **NOTICE THE GRAMMAR.** Look at Activity 1. Underline *was.* Circle *wasn't.*

Ask and answer questions with the past tense of *be*.

Yes/No Questions with the Past Tense of *Be*

Questions

Was/Were	Subject	
Was	I	late? at a movie? interesting? on time?
Were	you	
Was	he she it	
Were	we you they	

Short Answers

	Subject	was/were
Yes,	you	were.
	I	was.
	he she it	was.
	we you they	were.

	Subject	was/were + not
No,	you	weren't.
	I	wasn't.
	he she it	wasn't.
	we you they	weren't.

---

3 **WRITE.** Complete the conversation with *was, were, wasn't,* or *weren't.*

1. **A:** _____ Was _____ Ben at the beach yesterday?

   B: No, he _____. He was in class.

2. **A:** _____ Tina and Lily at a museum yesterday?

   B: Yes, they _____.

3. **A:** _____ you at an amusement park yesterday?

   B: Yes, I _____.

4. **A:** _____ it cold last week?

   B: No, it _____. It was warm.

5. **A:** _____ class interesting last week?

   B: No, it _____. It was boring.

4 **WHAT ABOUT YOU?** Answer the questions about you.

1. Were you in class yesterday? _____

2. Was your class fun yesterday? _____

3. Was your weekend relaxing? _____

4. Was work stressful last week? _____

TALK with a partner. Ask and answer the questions.

LESSON 5: Grammar Practice Plus

1 **WRITE.** Complete the sentences with *was* or *were*.

1 The traffic ___was___ **slow**.

2 The roads _____ **dangerous**.

3 The mountains _____ **beautiful**.

4 The boat _____ **fast**.

5 The lake _____ **clean**.

6 The hotel _____ **dirty**.

LISTEN and repeat. Are your answers correct?

TCD3, 33

2 **WHAT ABOUT YOU?** Write *Was* or *Were* to complete the questions. Answer the questions about your native country.

1. _____Was_____ your life stressful?

   Answer: _____

2. _____ your friends fun?

   Answer: _____

3. _____ your school beautiful?

   Answer: _____

4. _____ your neighborhood dangerous?

   Answer: _____

5. _____ your city near the mountains?

   Answer: _____

TALK with a partner. Ask and answer the questions.

3 **READ** the emails. <u>Underline</u> *was*, *wasn't*, *were*, and *weren't*.

heyyou.net

(2) Inbox	From: MariaG
Draft	Date: 10/3
(4) Sent	To: Dan037@heyyou.net
Bulk	Subject: What a vacation!
Trash	

Hi Dan,

I'm back from my vacation at the beach. It <u>was</u> great. The bus was clean and fast. The weather was sunny and warm. I liked everything. The vacation was both relaxing and exciting.

Talk to you soon.

Maria

heyyou.net

(6) Inbox	From: Dan
(1) Draft	Date: 10/4
(1) Sent	To: MariaG007@heyyou.net
Bulk	Subject: Lucky you
Trash	

Hi Maria,

Welcome back. I'm glad your vacation was good. Hugo and I weren't so lucky. The hotel was very dirty. Hugo was sick on the boat. It rained all the time. It was a little boring. Hugo and I were happy to go home.

Dan

4 **WRITE** questions about the emails. Use *was* or *were*.

1. Maria's vacation/terrible? _Was Maria's vacation terrible?_

2. Dan's vacation/boring? _____

3. Maria/happy/at the beach? _____

4. Dan and Hugo/happy to go home? _____

5. Dan/sick? _____

TALK with a partner. Ask and answer the questions.

Math: Understand Schedules

READ the train schedule. Compute how long each trip takes.

Train	Departs Oakland	Arrives San Jose	Fare	How long?
A	6:23 A.M.	7:35 A.M.	$14	*1 hour, 12 minutes*
B	7:10 A.M.	9:10 A.M.	$14	
C	8:50 A.M.	9:55 A.M.	$14	
D	8:53 A.M.	10:10 A.M.	$14	
E	12:03 P.M.	1:15 P.M.	$14	
F	7:33 P.M.	8:55 P.M.	$14	

LESSON 6: Apply Your Knowledge

1 **READ** the ads. Circle the places.

Fall Getaways

Come to the NC mountains!
See the fall colors at their
best.

Lake Vista Hotel
Downtown Brevard
(800) 555–FALL
Rooms $89–$159

This winter,
escape the cold.

*Florida is waiting
for you.*

San Fernandina Beach
Sun, swimming, smiles

**Call (800) 555-9000.
Only $159 a night**

Is life too fast?
Time slows down by
Lost Lake

Go for a walk, take a nap,
read a book.
This summer come
to the lake.
Call (800) 555-7722

TCD3, 34

2 **LISTEN.** Where did Susan go on vacation? Check ☑ the correct ad in Activity 1.

LISTEN AGAIN and complete the form.

Name: _____*Susan Miller*_____

Tell us what you think . . .

1. How was your vacation?

☐ terrible ☐ bad ☐ okay ☐ good ☐ excellent

2. How was your room? (Check all that are true.)

☐ large ☐ small

☐ clean ☐ dirty

☐ quiet ☐ noisy

3. How was the bus?

☐ fast ☐ slow ☐ clean ☐ dirty

Understand advertisements. • Complete a questionnaire.

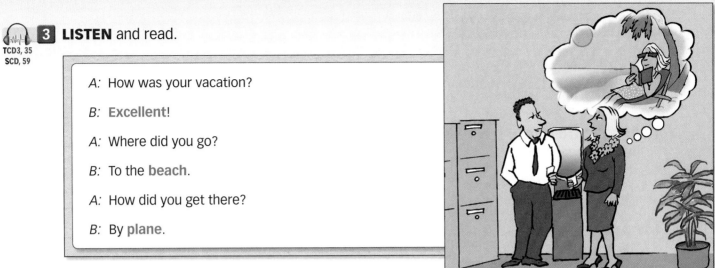

3 **LISTEN** and read.

TCD3, 35
SCD, 59

A: How was your vacation?

B: **Excellent**!

A: Where did you go?

B: To the **beach**.

A: How did you get there?

B: By **plane**.

LISTEN AGAIN and repeat. Then practice with a partner.

4 **PRACTICE THE CONVERSATION** with a partner.

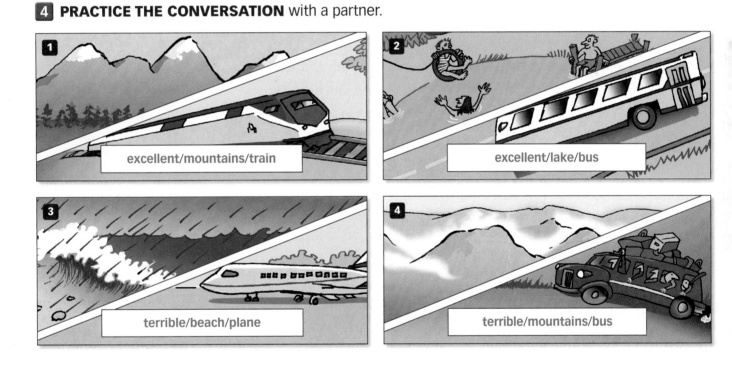

1 excellent/mountains/train

2 excellent/lake/bus

3 terrible/beach/plane

4 terrible/mountains/bus

5 **WHAT ABOUT YOU?** Complete the questionnaire about your last trip.

1. Where did you go? _____					
2. How did you get there?	☐ train	☐ plane	☐ bus	☐ car	☐ ship
3. How was the trip?	☐ terrible	☐ bad	☐ okay	☐ good	☐ excellent
4. How was the food?	☐ terrible	☐ bad	☐ okay	☐ good	☐ excellent
5. How was the weather?	☐ terrible	☐ bad	☐ okay	☐ good	☐ excellent

TALK with a partner about your trip.

LESSON 7: Reading

1 **THINK ABOUT IT.** What are some problems people have on vacations?

2 **BEFORE YOU READ.** Look at the story and picture. Check ☑ the problems.

☐ too hot   ☐ too rainy   ☐ too cold   ☐ too windy

3 **READ** the story. Write the definitions of *hurricane* and *shelter*.

> ### My Vacation
> #### By Anna Costello
>
> Last summer, I went to Florida on vacation with friends. In the beginning, the weather was very hot and sunny. It was relaxing, and we were happy. But then there was a hurricane. It rained and rained and was very windy. It was awful. The roads were dangerous, and there was no electricity. There were no trains, buses, or airplanes. We stayed in a shelter with many other people. It was very crowded and hot there, but it was safe. Finally, the hurricane ended, and we went home.

hurricane:_____

shelter: _____

4 **WRITE** sentences about Anna's vacation.

Place	Anna went to Florida.
Weather	
Problems	

Writing

1 **EDIT.** Read the story. Find three errors with *was/wasn't/were/weren't*. Correct the errors.

> Last winter, my family went to
> the mountains. The car ride ~~were~~ *was*
> long. At first, the weather were
> rainy and cold. We weren't happy.
> The vacation were boring. Then
> it snowed. We was very excited.
> After that, the vacation was fun.

2 **WRITE** five sentences about your trip. Use the simple past tense.

Writing Tip

Always edit your writing. Check for correct verb forms.

1. _____

2. _____

3. _____

4. _____

5. _____

3 **EDIT.** Work with a partner. Read your partner's sentences. Correct errors in the past tense form.

1. Last summer, my family ~~goed~~ *went* to the beach. _____

Career Connection

TCD3, 36

1 **READ** and listen. Then practice with a partner.

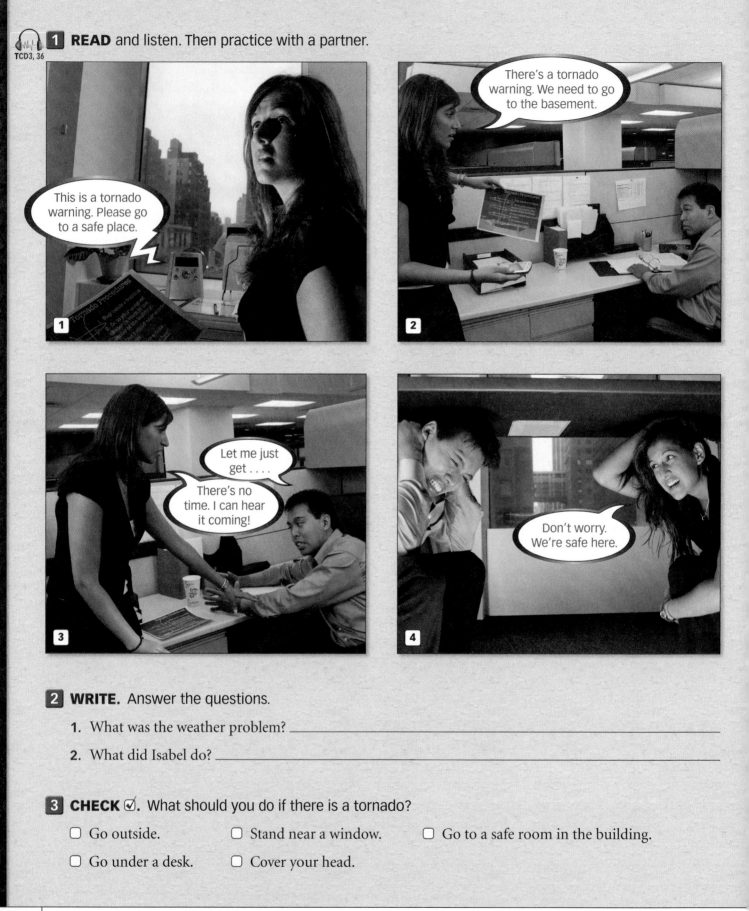

2 **WRITE.** Answer the questions.

1. What was the weather problem? _____

2. What did Isabel do? _____

3 **CHECK** ☑. What should you do if there is a tornado?

☐ Go outside.   ☐ Stand near a window.   ☐ Go to a safe room in the building.

☐ Go under a desk.   ☐ Cover your head.

Check Your Progress!

Skill	Circle the answer.	Is it correct?
A. Use the simple past of *be* in statements.	1. I **was** / **were** in Colombia in 1998. 2. He **wasn't** / **weren't** a doctor in 2002. 3. They **was** / **were** late yesterday.	○ ○ ○

		Number Correct	0	1	2	3

Skill	Circle the answer.	Is it correct?
B. Use simple past of *be* in questions and short answers.	4. **Did** / **Was** it rainy yesterday? 5. **Was** / **Were** you at home at 10 P.M.? 6. **Was** / **Were** she in class last week?	○ ○ ○

		Number Correct	0	1	2	3

Skill	Circle the answer.	Is it correct?
C. Talk about transportation.	7. The **train** / **platform** was fast. 8. The **bus** / **lake** was slow. 9. I'm sorry I missed the meeting. The train was **on time** / **late**.	○ ○ ○

		Number Correct	0	1	2	3

Skill	Circle the answer.	Is it correct?
D. Describe events and trips.	10. The movie was terrible. It was **boring** / **exciting**. 11. The beach was wonderful! It was **relaxing** / **stressful**. 12. Our trip wasn't good. It was **dangerous** / **interesting**.	○ ○ ○

		Number Correct	0	1	2	3

COUNT the number of correct answers above. Fill in the bubbles.

Chart Your Success				
Skill	Need more practice	Okay	Good	Excellent!
A. Use the simple past of *be* in statements.	⓪	①	②	③
B. Use simple past of *be* in questions and short answers.	⓪	①	②	③
C. Talk about transportation.	⓪	①	②	③
D. Describe events and trips.	⓪	①	②	③

LESSON 1: Grammar and Vocabulary

1 **GRAMMAR PICTURE DICTIONARY.** Listen and repeat.

TCD3, 37
SCD, 60

1. She has **the flu**.

2. They have **colds**.

3. He has **a fever**.

4. She has **a backache**.

5. She has **a headache**.

6. He has **a stomachache**.

7. She has **a sore throat**.

8. He has **a cough**.

9. They have **runny noses**.

2 **NOTICE THE GRAMMAR.** Look at Activity 1. Circle *have*. Underline *has*.

> The past tense of *have* is *had*. I **had** a headache yesterday.

Have for Health Problems

We use *have* to talk about health problems.

Affirmative Statements

Subject	*have/has*	Noun
I You	have	a headache.
He She	has	a fever.
We You They	have	colds.

Negative Statements

Subject	*don't/doesn't*	*have/has*	Noun
I You	don't		a headache.
He She	doesn't	have	a fever.
We You They	don't		colds.

3 **WRITE.** Complete the sentences. Use *have*, *has*, *don't have*, or *doesn't have*.

1. I _____*have*_____ a headache.

2. He _____ a cold.

3. We _____ (not) stomachaches.

4. You _____ a fever.

5. I _____ (not) a backache.

6. They _____ the flu.

7. She _____ (not) an earache.

8. David and Peter _____ coughs.

9. Maria _____ a toothache.

10. You _____ (not) a fever.

4 **GAME.** Work in a small group. Act out a health problem. Your classmates guess your problem.

LESSON 2: Grammar Practice Plus

1 WRITE. Complete the sentences. Use a word in the box.

back	ear	feet	hands	neck	stomach

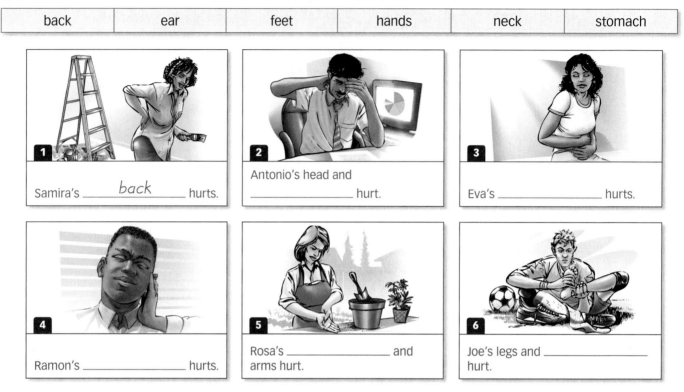

1. Samira's ___*back*___ hurts.

2. Antonio's head and _____ hurt.

3. Eva's _____ hurts.

4. Ramon's _____ hurts.

5. Rosa's _____ and arms hurt.

6. Joe's legs and _____ hurt.

 LISTEN and repeat. Are your answers correct?

TCD3, 38

2 WRITE. Complete the email. Use *have*, *has*, *hurt*, or *hurts*.

easymail.com   Welcome Liza! Sign out

[Check mail] [Compose] [Search mail] [_____] [Search the Web]

Inbox

Draft

Sent

Bulk

Trash

Upgrades
Options

To: g.hansen@mailtoyou.net;   **From:** liza.montgomery@easymail.com;
Subject: Ugh . . .
Date: 7-12, 4:32 p.m.

Hi Gwen,

How are you? I'm not feeling very well. I _____ the flu. My stomach _____,
                                            1   2
and my head _____. My two sisters _____ the flu, too. They are very sick.
                        3   4
They _____ headaches and stomachaches. Their backs _____, too.
     5   6

I hope you are healthy! Write soon.

Liza

---

168 | Identify parts of the body. • Use *have* to describe ailments.

3 **TALK** about the picture.

4 **LISTEN** and complete the sentences.

1. Elena has a _____.

2. Eliza's _____ hurt.

3. Alex has a _____.

4. Gloria's _____ hurts.

5. Luis has a _____.

6. Ibrahim has a _____.

5 **WRITE** the names next to the people in the picture.

6 **TALK** to a partner. Say how the people feel.

LESSON 3: Listening and Conversation

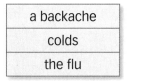

TCD3, 40

1 **LISTEN.** Complete the sentences. Use the words in the box.

1. Elga has ___the flu___.

2. Jung and her family have _____.

3. Richard has _____.

a backache
colds
the flu

LISTEN AGAIN. Check ☑ the body parts that hurt.

Elga

- ☐ head
- ☐ back
- ☐ stomach
- ☐ throat
- ☐ ears

Jung and her family

- ☐ head
- ☐ back
- ☐ stomach
- ☐ throat
- ☐ ears

Richard

- ☐ head
- ☐ back
- ☐ stomach
- ☐ throat
- ☐ ears

TCD3, 41–43

2 **LISTEN** to the conversations. Complete the messages.

While You Were Out

Name: _Radek_

Time: _8:35 A.M._

Date: _3/24_

Message: _He has_ _____

_____

_____

_____

While You Were Out

Name: _Patricia_

Time: _____

Date: _____

Message: _She can't come_

to work. She has a cold

and a headache.

_____

_____

While You Were Out

Name: _Audrey_

Time: _____

Date: _5/19_

Message: _She has a_

terrible _____.

She can't _____.

_____

_____

3 **LISTEN** and read.

TCD3, 44
SCD, 61

A: Hello?

B: Hi, this is **John**. I'm sick. I can't come to work today.

A: Oh, what's wrong?

B: I have a **sore throat** and a **runny nose**. I feel terrible!

A: That's too bad. Get well soon.

B: Thanks.

LISTEN AGAIN and repeat. Then practice with a partner.

4 **PRACTICE THE CONVERSATION** with a partner.

Ann

Joe

Dennis

Rita

Boris

Tracy

5 **WRITE.** You are sick. You can't go to class. You call your teacher. Write the conversation.

TALK. Practice your conversation with a partner.

LESSON 4: Grammar and Vocabulary

1 **GRAMMAR PICTURE DICTIONARY.** Listen and repeat.

TCD3, 45
SCD, 62

1 Lisa has the flu.

She should (rest.)

She should **drink liquids**.

2 Bill's back hurts.

He should **use a heating pad**.

He should **get a prescription** for a pain reliever.

3 Isha's fingers hurt.

She should **put ice on them**.

She should **put on a bandage**.

4 They were in a car accident.

She should **call 911**.

EXAM ROOM 1

He should **see a doctor**.

2 **NOTICE THE GRAMMAR.** Look at Activity 1. Underline *should*. (Circle) the verb.

Give advice with *should*. • Describe remedies.

Should for Advice

We use *should* to give advice or say that something is a good idea.

Statements		
Subject	***should/shouldn't***	**Verb**
I You He She We You They	should shouldn't	rest.

Questions		
should	**Subject**	**Verb**
Should	I you he she we you they	rest?

Answers		
Yes/No	**Subject**	***should/shouldn't***
Yes, No,	you I he she we you they	should. shouldn't.

3 WRITE. Complete the sentences with *should* or *shouldn't*.

1. Rafael's foot hurts. He _____*shouldn't*_____ play soccer.

2. I have a bad earache. I _____ see a doctor.

3. Lydia's leg hurts. She _____ use a heating pad.

4. Mario and Martha have headaches. They _____ rest.

5. You have a fever. You _____ go to school.

4 WHAT ABOUT YOU? Choose a health problem. Ask a partner for advice. Check ☑ your partner's answers.

I have _____.
(health problem)

1. Should I rest? ☐ Yes, you should. ☐ No, you shouldn't.

2. Should I see a doctor? ☐ Yes, you should. ☐ No, you shouldn't.

3. Should I take medicine? ☐ Yes, you should. ☐ No, you shouldn't.

4. Should I put on a bandage? ☐ Yes, you should. ☐ No, you shouldn't.

5. Should I use a heating pad? ☐ Yes, you should. ☐ No, you shouldn't.

6. Should I call 911? ☐ Yes, you should. ☐ No, you shouldn't.

7. Should I drink liquids? ☐ Yes, you should. ☐ No, you shouldn't.

8. Should I go to English class? ☐ Yes, you should. ☐ No, you shouldn't.

LESSON 5: Grammar Practice Plus

1 MATCH.

a. pain reliever

b. ~~cough medicine~~

c. throat lozenge

d. ear drops

1. Mark has a cold. He should take ___*b*___.

2. Musa has an earache. He should use _____.

3. Ellen's head hurts. She should take a _____.

4. Tina has a sore throat. She should take a _____.

LISTEN and repeat. Are your answers correct?

TCD3, 46

Pronunciation: *Should* and *Shouldn't*

A **LISTEN** and repeat.

TCD3, 47
SCD, 63

1. You should stay in bed. You shouldn't go to work.

2. She should use a heating pad. She shouldn't put ice on it.

B **LISTEN.** Circle *should* or *shouldn't*.

TCD3, 48
SCD, 64

1. Marco **should** / (**shouldn't**) call 911.

2. Henry **should** / **shouldn't** take cough medicine.

3. Sara **should** / **shouldn't** stay in bed.

4. Gloria **should** / **shouldn't** use ear drops.

C **TALK.** Read the sentences to a partner.

---

2 WRITE the words in the chart.

Problems	Remedies
flu	*sleep*

a backache	ear drops	rest
bandage	~~flu~~	~~sleep~~
cold	headache	sore throat
cough	heating pad	stomachache
cough medicine	ice	throat lozenge
drink liquids	pain reliever	fever

3 **WRITE** advice for each person. Use remedies from the chart in Activity 2.

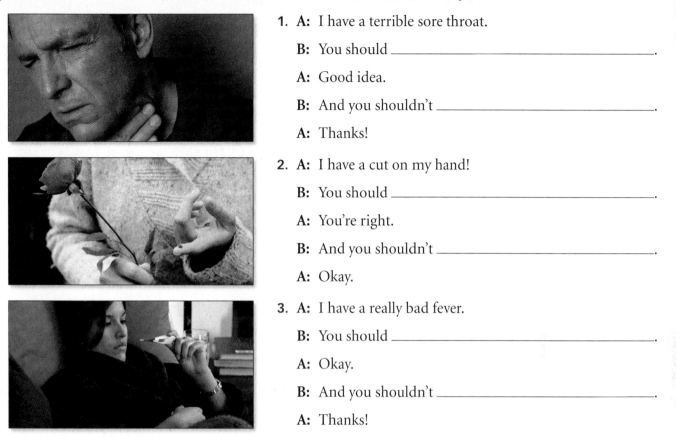

1. **A:** I have a terrible sore throat.

   B: You should _____.

   A: Good idea.

   B: And you shouldn't _____.

   A: Thanks!

2. **A:** I have a cut on my hand!

   B: You should _____.

   A: You're right.

   B: And you shouldn't _____.

   A: Okay.

3. **A:** I have a really bad fever.

   B: You should _____.

   A: Okay.

   B: And you shouldn't _____.

   A: Thanks!

TALK. Practice the conversations with a partner.

Math: Medicine Labels

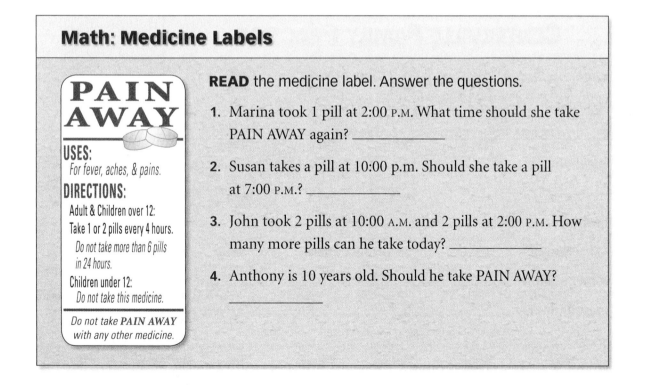

PAIN AWAY

USES:
For fever, aches, & pains.

DIRECTIONS:
Adult & Children over 12:
Take 1 or 2 pills every 4 hours.
  Do not take more than 6 pills
  in 24 hours.
Children under 12:
  Do not take this medicine.

Do not take **PAIN AWAY**
with any other medicine.

READ the medicine label. Answer the questions.

1. Marina took 1 pill at 2:00 P.M. What time should she take PAIN AWAY again? _____

2. Susan takes a pill at 10:00 p.m. Should she take a pill at 7:00 P.M.? _____

3. John took 2 pills at 10:00 A.M. and 2 pills at 2:00 P.M. How many more pills can he take today? _____

4. Anthony is 10 years old. Should he take PAIN AWAY? _____

LESSON 6: Apply Your Knowledge

1 **READ** the appointment card and insurance card. Circle:

1. The time of the appointment
2. The patient's name
3. The policy number
4. The group number

CENTERVILLE FAMILY PRACTICE

Patient: _Carlos Rodriguez_

☐ Mon ☐ Tue ☐ Wed ☐ Thu ☑ Fri ☐ Sat

Date: _7/28_   Time: (1:45 P.M.)

Doctor: _Lopez_

Excellent Health Insurance

Policy Number: 108407
Group Number: ATL1948
Smith Construction Co.
Customer Service: 1.800.632.9276

TCD3, 49

2 **LISTEN** to the conversation. Complete the sentences.

1. Carlos's appointment is on _Friday, July 28_ .

2. Carlos's phone number is _____.

3. The reason for Carlos's visit is _____.

3 **WRITE.** Complete the Patient Information Form. Use the information in Activities 1 and 2.

CENTERVILLE FAMILY PRACTICE

Name: _Carlos Rodriguez_   **Date of Birth:** _7/5/62_

Address: _4972 Brown Street_
Street
Centerville   _New York_   _14025_
City   State   Zip Code

Telephone: _973-1265_   _977-9241_
Home   Work

Insurance: _Excellent Health Insurance_

Policy Number: _____   **New Patient:**   Yes   No

Doctor's Name: _____

Reason for Visit: _____

_____

_____

TCD3, 50
SCD, 65

4 **LISTEN** and read.

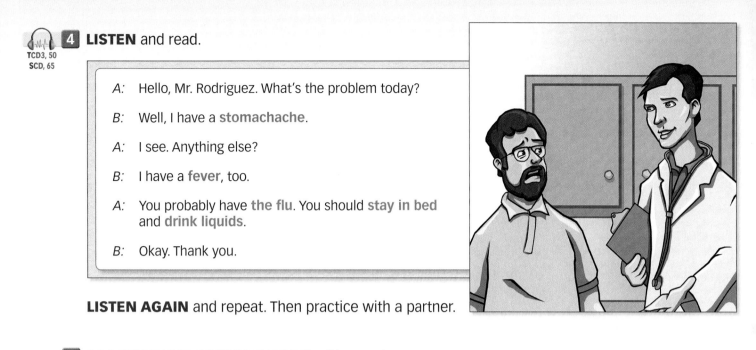

A: Hello, Mr. Rodriguez. What's the problem today?

B: Well, I have a **stomachache**.

A: I see. Anything else?

B: I have a **fever**, too.

A: You probably have **the flu**. You should **stay in bed** and **drink liquids**.

B: Okay. Thank you.

LISTEN AGAIN and repeat. Then practice with a partner.

5 **PRACTICE THE CONVERSATION** with a partner.

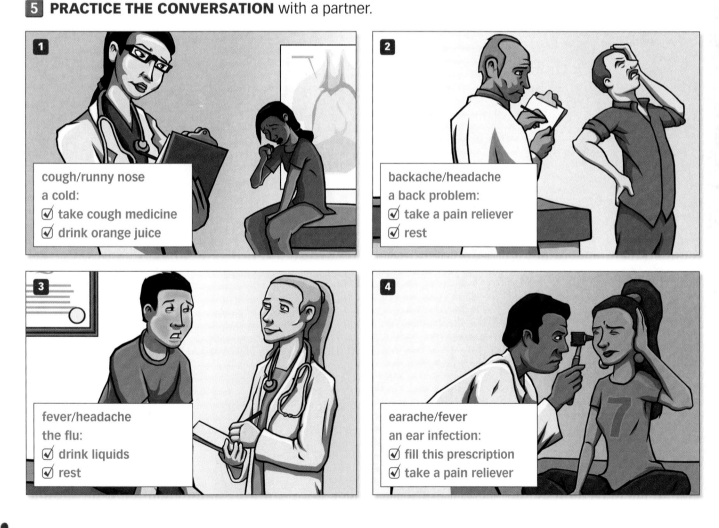

1
cough/runny nose
a cold:
☑ take cough medicine
☑ drink orange juice

2
backache/headache
a back problem:
☑ take a pain reliever
☑ rest

3
fever/headache
the flu:
☑ drink liquids
☑ rest

4
earache/fever
an ear infection:
☑ fill this prescription
☑ take a pain reliever

6 **WHAT ABOUT YOU?** Tell a partner about a health problem you or a family member has. Your partner gives advice.

LESSON 7: Reading

1 **THINK ABOUT IT.** What do you do to be healthy?

2 **BEFORE YOU READ.** Look at the pictures. What words can you say about each picture?

3 **READ** the article. What is it about? Circle the answer.

   A. Good health is not important.

   B. Good food is not important to good health.

   C. There are five important things you should do for good health.

Reading Tip

Before you read, look at the pictures. The pictures can help you understand new words.

Keys to Good Health

There are five keys to good health.

- First, eat right. You should eat breakfast, lunch, and dinner every day. It is important to eat lots of fruit and vegetables. You shouldn't eat much junk food, such as hamburgers and French fries.

- Second, brush and floss your teeth every day.

- Third, exercise is important. You should walk or run for 20 minutes every day.

- Next, drink lots of water, especially in hot weather.

- Last, relax. You should learn to relax and rest. Go out and sit in the park. Close your eyes and don't think about work.

Do all these things for a healthy life.

4 **MATCH** the word with the definition.

   ___d___ **1.** junk food   **a.** activities or sports to improve your body's health

   _____ **2.** floss   **b.** sit or rest

   _____ **3.** exercise   **c.** clean between your teeth

   _____ **4.** relax   **d.** food that is not good for your health

5 **WRITE** the five keys to good health.

   1. _____*Eat fruits and vegetables.*_____   **4.** _____

   2. _____   **5.** _____

   3. _____

Writing

1 **READ.** Look at the paragraph below. Underline the first sentence. Circle the space before the first word.

2 **READ** the paragraph. Underline the things Mike should do for good health.

indent ⟶ For good health, I should do many things. I should eat vegetables and fruit every day, and I shouldn't eat potato chips. I should drink water. I shouldn't drink coffee and soda. I should floss my teeth. I should eat healthy food and exercise. Then I can have a healthy life.

—Mike Burns

3 **WHAT ABOUT YOU?** What should you do for good health? Write four sentences.

To improve my health, I should do many things…

1. _____

2. _____

3. _____

4. _____

4 **WRITE** your sentences from Activity 3 in a paragraph.

_____

_____

_____

_____

_____

_____

_____

Career Connection

TCD3, 51

1 READ and listen. Then practice with a partner.

2 TALK ABOUT IT. Answer the questions.

1. What was the problem with Isabel's boss?

2. What did Isabel do?

3. What advice does her boss have for Isabel?

3 WHAT ABOUT YOU? Think of a time you helped someone or did a good job. What did you do? What did the person think?

Check Your Progress!

Skill	Circle the answer.	Is it correct?
A. Use the present with *have*.	1. Bima and Elga **have** / **has** the flu. 2. Alex **have** / **has** a headache. 3. Claudia and her sisters **have** / **has** colds.	☐ ☐ ☐

		Number Correct	0	1	2	3

Skill	Circle the answer.	Is it correct?
B. Describe symptoms.	4. My mother has a cold. Her **head** / **arms** hurts. 5. I was in a car accident. My **throat** / **back** hurts. 6. The children have the flu. Their **stomachs** / **feet** hurt.	☐ ☐ ☐

		Number Correct	0	1	2	3

Skill	Circle the answer.	Is it correct?
C. Use *should* to give advice.	7. Paul was in an accident. He **should to take** / **should take** a pain reliever. 8. My sister has a cut. **Should she use** / **She should use** a bandage? 9. Jane has a backache. She **should not take** / **not should take** cough medicine.	☐ ☐ ☐

		Number Correct	0	1	2	3

Skill	Circle the answer.	Is it correct?
D. Talk about remedies.	10. Patricia and Matt have coughs. They should take **a pain reliever** / **cough medicine**. 11. Gloria's hand hurts. She should **put ice on it** / **drink liquids**. 12. Tim has a fever. He should **put on a bandage** / **see a doctor**.	☐ ☐ ☐

		Number Correct	0	1	2	3

COUNT the number of correct answers above. Fill in the bubbles.

Chart Your Success

Skill	Need more practice	Okay	Good	Excellent!
A. Use the present with *have*.	⓪	①	②	③
B. Describe symptoms.	⓪	①	②	③
C. Use *should* to give advice.	⓪	①	②	③
D. Talk about remedies.	⓪	①	②	③

LESSON 1: Grammar and Vocabulary

1 **GRAMMAR PICTURE DICTIONARY.** Listen and repeat.

TCD3, 52
SCD, 66

Next week ...

1 Tim is going to start a new job.

2 Beth is going to **ask for a raise**.

3 Julia is going to **have a baby**.

Next month ...

4 Jane is going to **finish school**.

5 Jane and Scott are going to **get married**.

6 They are going to **go on a honeymoon**.

Next year ...

7 Peter is going to **sell his house**.

8 He is going to **move to a new city**.

9 He is going to **rent an apartment**.

2 **NOTICE THE GRAMMAR.** Look at Activity 1. Underline *is/are going to*. Circle the verb.

Future With *Be Going To*

We use *be going to* to talk about:
- Future plans. (I'm **going to** get married this summer.)
- Things we can see are going to happen soon. (Look at those clouds! It's **going to** rain.)

Affirmative Statements

Subject	be	going to	Verb
I	am		
You	are		
He She	is	going to	move.
We You They	are		

Negative Statements

Subject	be	not	going to	Verb
I	am			
You	are			
He She	is	not	going to	move.
We You They	are			

3 **WRITE.** Complete the sentences with the correct form of *be going to* + verb.

1. Raquel _____*is going to move*_____ (move) to New York next month.

2. Raul and Michael _____ (finish) school next week.

3. Sara and I _____ (not rent) an apartment together.

4. My husband and I _____ (visit) our friends this weekend.

5. James _____ (not sell) his car.

6. I _____ (ask) for a raise this year.

7. They _____ (eat) in a restaurant tomorrow.

8. She _____ (watch) TV tonight.

4 **WHAT ABOUT YOU?** Complete the sentences about *you*. Use *be going to*.

1. Tonight, I _____.

2. This weekend, I _____.

3. Next week, I _____.

4. Next month, I _____.

TALK. Read your sentences to a partner.

This weekend, I'm going to study English.

LESSON 2: Grammar Practice Plus

Object Pronouns

Subject Pronouns	Object Pronouns
I	me
you	you
he	him
she	her
it	it
we	us
you	you
they	them

Subject	Verb	Object Pronoun
She He	likes	me. you. him. her. it. us. you. them.

---

1 **WRITE.** Look at Julie's calendar. Correct the sentences. Use object pronouns.

Sunday	Monday	Tuesday	Wednesday	Thursday	Friday	Saturday
11 Family party	12 Call landlord (Ms. Smith)	13	14 Finish class	15	16	17 Get married!
18 Honeymoon ——————	19	20	21	22	23	24 Friends help us move

1. Julie is going to finish her class on ~~May 13~~.

   Julie is going to finish it on May 14.

2. Their friends are going to help Ben and Julie move on May 23.

   _____

3. Julie is going to marry Ben on May 18.

   _____

4. Julie is going to call Ms. Smith on May 13.

   _____

2 **TALK** about the picture.

3 **MATCH.**

_____c_____ **1.** Ben and Julie   **a.** is going to sit down.

_____ **2.** Mary   **b.** isn't going to drive the car.

_____ **3.** Leyla   ~~**c.** are going to get married.~~

_____ **4.** Thomas   **d.** is going to have a baby.

_____ **5.** Joe   **e.** is going to help John.

4 **TALK** with a partner. What is going to happen next?
Use your own ideas.

1. Ella   **3.** Thomas

2. Jacob and Sara   **4.** Leyla

LESSON **3**: Listening and Conversation

Pronunciation: *Going To (Gonna)*

We often pronounce *going to* **as** *gonna*. **We don't usually write** *gonna*.

LISTEN for the pronunciation of *going to*.

TCD3, 53
SCD, 67

1. James and Linda are going to get married!

2. What are they going to do after the wedding?

3. They're going to go on their honeymoon.

4. They're going to move to a new apartment.

1 **LISTEN** and number the pictures.

TCD3, 54

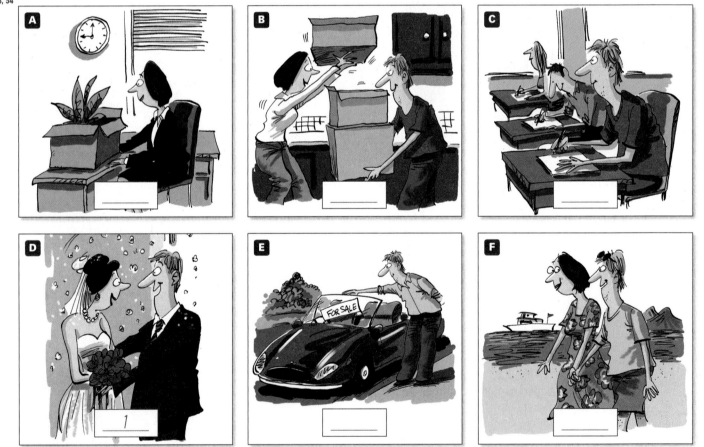

2 **TALK.** Tell a partner about James' and Linda's plans.

Interpret a timeline. • Ask for help.

 LISTEN and read.

TCD3, 55
SCD, 68

A: Do you have plans for this weekend?

B: I'm going to **pay the bills** Saturday morning. Why?

A: Well… I'm going to **wash the car** in the afternoon. Can you help me?

B: Sure!

LISTEN AGAIN and repeat. Then practice with a partner.

4 **PRACTICE THE CONVERSATION** with a partner.

1. do my homework/fix the car
2. go to my sister's house/ pay the bills
3. clean the apartment/ fix the toilet
4. go to class/ paint the apartment
5. play soccer/fix the computer
6. go shopping/study English

5 **WHAT ABOUT YOU?** Write about your plans for the next six months.

I'm going to …	I'm not going to …
Example: *I'm going to finish school.*	**Example:** *I'm going to start a new job.*

TALK. Read your sentences to a partner.

LESSON 4: Grammar and Vocabulary

1 **GRAMMAR PICTURE DICTIONARY.** Listen and repeat.

1

A: Are you going to call the **phone company** today?

B: Yes, I am.

2

A: Are you going to order **cable television**?

B: Yes, we are.

3

A: Are you going to order **Internet access**?

B: No, we're not.

4

A: Are you going to buy a new **sofa**?

B: No, we like this one!

5

A: Is James going to fix this **bed**?

B: Yes, he is.

6

A: Are you going to paint this **dresser**?

B: Yes, we are.

7

A: Is the landlord going to buy a new **refrigerator**?

B: No, he's going to fix the old one.

8

A: Is your landlord going to fix the **dishwasher**?

B: No, he's going to call a plumber.

9

A: Is James going to install the new **microwave**?

B: No, he isn't. I am.

2 **NOTICE THE GRAMMAR.** Look at Activity 1. Circle *am*, *is*, or *are*. Underline the subject.

Questions With *Be Going To*

> She's not. = She isn't.
> We're not. = We aren't.

Questions

be	Subject	*going to*	Verb	
Am	I			
Are	you	going to	paint	the living room?
Is	he / she			
Are	we / you / they		rent	the apartment?

Answers

Yes, you are.	No, you're not.
Yes, I am.	No, I'm not.
Yes, he is.	No, he's not.
Yes, she is.	No, she's not.
Yes, you are.	No, you aren't.
Yes, we are.	No, we're not.
Yes, they are.	No, they're not.

---

3 **MATCH** the questions with the answers.

_b_ **1.** Are you going to call the landlord?

_____ **2.** Are they going to buy a new microwave?

_____ **3.** Is the landlord going to fix the refrigerator?

_____ **4.** Is Linda going to fix the dishwasher?

_____ **5.** Are we going to get cable TV?

a. Yes, we are. I'm going to call the cable company this weekend.

~~**b.** Yes, I am. I'm going to call him tomorrow.~~

c. No. They're going to use their old one.

d. Yes, he is. He's going to fix it next week.

e. No, she's not. The landlord is going to call a plumber.

TALK. Ask and answer the questions with a partner.

4 **WHAT ABOUT YOU?** Walk around the room and talk to your classmates. Complete the chart.

Are you going to …	Classmate's Name
1. move next year?	
2. start a new job this year?	
3. fix something this month?	
4. rent a new apartment this year?	
5. paint a room this month?	
6. visit a friend this weekend?	

> Are you going to move next year?

> No, I'm not.

LESSON 5: Grammar Practice Plus

1 **LISTEN** and repeat.

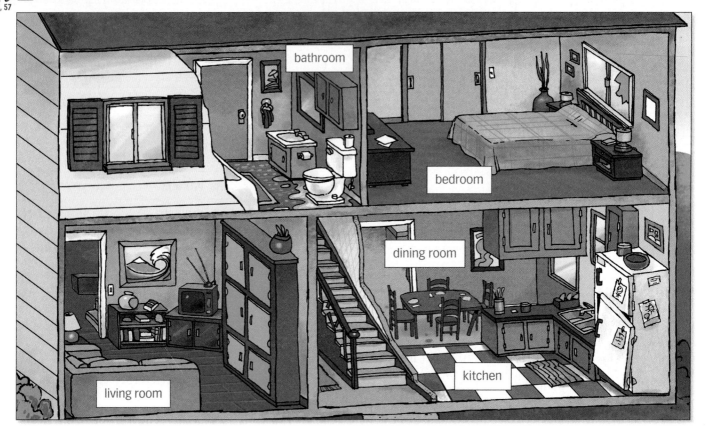

2 **WRITE.** Put the words in order to make questions.

1. a plumber / going to / Is / fix the toilet?

   _____ ☐ Yes ☐ No

2. Are / going to / carpenters / fix the stairs?

   _____ ☐ Yes ☐ No

3. carpenters / fix the cabinets / in the living room? / Are / going to

   _____ ☐ Yes ☐ No

4. Is / the landlord / fix the window / going to / in the bedroom?

   _____ ☐ Yes ☐ No

5. in the dining room? / Is / the landlord / paint the walls / going to

   _____ ☐ Yes ☐ No

3 **LISTEN** to Linda's conversation with her landlord. Check ☑ *Yes* or *No* above.

4 WRITE. Complete the chart. Use the words in the box.

bed	~~cabinets~~	cable TV	sofa
dishwasher	table	walls	carpet

Our House Plans			
Room	Jobs for James	Jobs for Linda	Jobs for James and Linda
dining room	fix the _____ and chairs	fix the window	paint the _____
living room	clean the _____	call the _____ company	fix the _cabinets_
kitchen	fix the refrigerator	buy a _____	clean the microwave
bedroom	fix the _____	vacuum the _____	paint the dresser

5 TALK with a partner. Look at the chart in Activity 4. Use the words below.
Ask and answer questions about James and Linda.

1. James and Linda / paint the walls in the dining room

2. Linda / buy a refrigerator

3. James / clean the sofa

4. James and Linda / paint the walls in the living room

5. Linda / vacuum the carpet

6. James / call the cable TV company

Are James and Linda going to paint the walls in the dining room?

Yes, they are.

6 WHAT ABOUT YOU? Write your plans for this week. Ask your classmates if they are going to do the same things.

My Plans for this Week
• _do my homework tomorrow_
•
•
•
•

I'm going to do my homework tomorrow. Are you going to do your homework?

Yes, I'm going to do it tonight.

LESSON 6: Apply Your Knowledge

1 **READ** the ads. In each ad, underline one thing you like.

BEAUTIFUL APARTMENT FOR RENT	HOUSE FOR RENT	AFFORDABLE APARTMENTS!
2 bedrooms, 1 bath, new kitchen and carpet. $850 a month. Call (619) 555–9821.	Big dining room and living room. 3 bedrooms, 2 bath. Big closets. Garage. $1,000/month.	1 bedroom, 1 bath. Kitchen and living room. No dining room. $650/month.

TCD3, 59

2 **LISTEN** to the conversation. Circle the ad in Activity 1 for the place that Paula is going to rent.

LISTEN AGAIN. Check ☑ the things with problems.

- ☐ kitchen cabinets
- ☐ stairs
- ☐ bathroom sink
- ☐ windows
- ☐ dishwasher
- ☐ carpet
- ☐ paint
- ☐ refrigerator
- ☐ microwave

Math Review: Add and Subtract

Paula is going to fix and change a lot of things in her house. Look at the list of plans and costs. Answer the questions.

Paula's Plans	
Paint the living room	$500
Paint the cabinets in the bathroom	$400
Clean the bedroom carpet	$150
Buy a new refrigerator	$750
Fix the stairs	$350
Fix the dishwasher	$200

1. How much is Paula going to pay to fix the stairs? _____

2. How much is it going to cost to fix all the problems? _____

3. How much is Paula going to spend on the kitchen? _____

4. The landlord is going to pay for $1,000 of the cost. How much is Paula going to pay? _____

3 **LISTEN** and read.

TCD3, 60
SCD, 70

A: I'm going to **go to the museum** tomorrow.
Do you want to come?

B: Sorry, I can't. I'm going to work on my apartment.

A: Really? What are you going to do?

B: **Fix the kitchen cabinets.**

A: Oh, okay. Maybe next time?

B: Sure! Thanks!

LISTEN AGAIN and repeat. Then practice with a partner.

4 **PRACTICE THE CONVERSATION** with a partner.

1 study at the library/
fix the toilet

2 drive to the beach/
install a dishwasher

3 go shopping/
clean the kitchen

4 go to the movies/
paint the dining room

5 walk in the park/
paint the kitchen cabinets

6 look for a new car/
fix the stairs

5 **TALK.** Invite your partner
to do something this weekend.

I'm going to go to the movies on Saturday night. Do you want to come?

Sorry, I can't. I'm going to study English.

LESSON 7: Reading

1 THINK ABOUT IT. What part of your life do you want to change?

☐ family   ☐ job   ☐ school

2 BEFORE YOU READ. Look at the title. What is the article about?

☐ Change is difficult.   ☐ Change is easy.

Reading Tip

Before you read, look at the title. The title helps you understand the reading.

3 READ. Underline the three steps to change.

EASY STEPS TO CHANGE

All people want to change something in their lives. What do you want to change? Your family life? Your job? School? Use these three easy steps:

1. First, write about the problem. For example, write names of people or activities.

2. Next, think about ways to fix the problem. Write a list of:

- people who can help you
- places you can get more information
- times and days you can work on the problem

For example, Luke Madsen wants to get a new job. Luke wrote, "I'm going to ask a career counselor for help."

3. Last, start to change. Call the people or go to the places on your list. You can do it!

4 WRITE. Look at the article. What are the three steps to change something in your life?

1. _First,_ _____

2. _____

3. _____

Predict the content of a text from the title.

Writing

Writing Tip

Examples make your writing interesting.

1 **WRITE.** What are your plans? Complete the chart.

My plan for change: *Learn more English.*

People I can ask for help	Places to get information	Days/times to work on the problem
my teacher	*the library*	*Mondays, 9:00 A.M.*

2 **WRITE** sentences about your plans.

Example: *I'm going to talk to my teacher.*

1. ______
2. ______
3. ______
4. ______

3 **WRITE** your sentences as a paragraph.

I'm going to ______

Career Connection

1 READ AND LISTEN. Then practice with a partner.

1. How's school, Isabel?

It's great!

2. I'm taking a class about medicine and prescriptions.

Interesting!

3. Yes... and it's my last class! I'm going to finish school next month!

Already?

4. Congratulations, Isabel!

Thank you!

2 TALK. Answer the questions.

1. What class is Isabel taking?

2. When is Isabel going to finish school?

3. How does Isabel feel?

3 WHAT ABOUT YOU? Make a list of your plans for your future.

- *I am going to* _____

- _____

- _____

- _____

- _____

Check Your Progress!

Skill	Circle the answer.	Is it correct?
A. Use future with *be going to*.	1. Ana and Tim **is going to** / **aren't going to** move this weekend. 2. Liza **is going to** / **is going** change jobs. 3. Joseph **not is going to** / **is not going to** sell his car.	☐ ☐ ☐
		Number Correct 0 1 2 3
B. Talk about activities.	4. Manuel doesn't make much money. He's going to **ask for a raise** / **rent an apartment**. 5. Tara has a new computer. She is going **to buy** / **sell** her old computer. 6. Paul is going to change jobs. He and his family are going to **move to a new city** / **get married**.	☐ ☐ ☐
		Number Correct 0 1 2 3
C. Ask questions with *be going to*.	7. **Are** / **Is** Sandra and Bill going to get married? 8. **Am** / **Is** I going to finish school this year? 9. **Are** / **Is** Kate going to have a baby?	☐ ☐ ☐
		Number Correct 0 1 2 3
D. Talk about housing.	10. I'm going to take a shower in the **kitchen** / **bathroom**. 11. My family is going to eat dinner in the **bedroom** / **dining room**. 12. We're going to buy a new **dresser** / **microwave** for the bedroom.	☐ ☐ ☐
		Number Correct 0 1 2 3

COUNT the number of correct answers above. Fill in the bubbles.

Chart Your Success				
Skill	Need more practice	Okay	Good	Excellent!
A. Use future with *be going to*.	⓪	①	②	③
B. Talk about activities.	⓪	①	②	③
C. Ask questions with *be going to*.	⓪	①	②	③
D. Talk about housing.	⓪	①	②	③

Information Gap Activity

UNIT 6

LESSON 5
Activity 3, page 95

Student B: Look at the picture below. Point to the pictures and talk with your partner. Write the prices of the clothes.

Grammar Reference Guide

Nouns

Singular and Plural Nouns

Singular (1)		Article	Singular Noun
Use *a* before singular nouns that start with a consonant (b, c, d, f, g, h, j, k, l, m, n, p, q, r, s, t, v, w, x, y, z)	I am He is	a	waiter. ——— consonants firefighter.
Use *an* before singular nouns that start with a vowel (a, e, i, o, and u).	You are	an	——— vowel office assistant.

Plural (2+)		Plural Noun
Add *s* to most nouns to make the nouns plural.	They are We are You are	waiters. firefighters. office assistants.

Possessives of Nouns

Add 's to make a noun possessive.

Ann	Ann's	I am Ann's brother.
the teacher	the teacher's	Mrs. Green is the teacher's wife.

> Non-count nouns use *is*.
> *Rice is good.*

Count and Non-Count Nouns

We count some nouns (*1, 2, 3 apples*). We don't count other nouns (*milk, water*).

Count Nouns		Non-count Nouns
Article + Singular Noun	Plural Noun	
a carrot an apple	carrots apples	milk cheese

Object Pronouns

Subject Pronouns	Object Pronouns
I	me
you	you
he	him
she	her
it	it
we	us
you	you
they	them

Subject	Verb	Object Pronoun
She He	likes	me. you. him. her. it. us. you. them.

Adjectives

Possessive Adjectives

Subject	Possessive Adjective	Examples
I	my	**My** name is Mara Lane.
you	your	This is **your** teacher.
he	his	**His** sister is pretty.
she	her	**Her** daughters are Linda and Pam.
we	our	Henry is **our** son.
you	your	**Your** brother is handsome.
they	their	**Their** mother is hardworking.

Prepositions

Prepositions of Location

We use prepositions to tell locations.

We use *at* with addresses and *home, school,* and *work*.

	Preposition	
There is an office	at	42 Pine Street. school.

We use *in* with names of buildings or rooms.

The snack bar is	in	room 206. the Harper Building.

We use *on* with floors of a building or streets.

The library is	on	the second floor. Main Street.

Prepositions of Location

We use prepositions to tell locations.

1 across from	**2** next to	**3** in front of	**4** behind	**5** between

Noun	*be*	Preposition	Noun(s)
The bank		next to	the supermarket.
The library	is	between	the school and the post office.
The school		across from	the drugstore.
The houses	are	behind	the school.

Present, Past, and Future Verb Forms

We use contractions (*I'm*) more than long forms (*I am*).

Affirmative Statements With *Be*

We use the verb *to be (am, is, are)* with personal information.

Subject	*be*			Contractions
I	am			I am = I'm
You	are	married.		You are = You're
He		single.		He is = He's
She	is	from China.		She is = She's
It				It is = It's

We		students.		We are = We're
You	are	married.		You are = You're
They		from India.		They are = They're

Negative Statements With *Be*

Subject	*be*	*not*		Contractions
I	am		a student.	I am not = I'm not
You	are		a teacher.	You are not = You're not/you aren't
He				He is not = He's not/He isn't
She	is	not	from China.	She is not = She's not/She isn't
It				It is not = It's not/It isn't
We			from Mexico.	We are not = We're not/We aren't
You	are		married.	You are not = You're not/You aren't
They			students.	They are not = They're not/They aren't

Yes/No Questions with *Be*

We use *be* with adjectives.

Questions

Be	Subject	Adjective
Am	I	
Are	you	
Is	he / she	funny? messy? shy?
Are	we / you / they	

Answers

	Subject	*be*			Subject	*be + not*
Yes,	you	are.		No,	you	aren't.
	I	am.			I	'm not.
	he / she / it	is.			he / she / it	isn't.
	we / you / they	are.			we / you / they	aren't.

How Much Questions with *Be*

We ask *How much* to learn the cost of something.

Questions

How much	*be*	Noun
How much	is	the purple dress? the black jacket?
	are	the blue shoes? the yellow jackets?

Answers

It's / They're	Noun
It's	twenty-five dollars. thirty-seven dollars. fifteen dollars.
They're	

What Time and *When* Questions with *Be*

Questions			Answers
Question Word	*be*	**Noun**	
What time	is	it?	It's 9:30 A.M. It's 12:00 P.M.
What time	is	your English class?	It's at 9:00 A.M.
When	are	the classes?	They're at 2:00 P.M. and 3:00 P.M.
When	is	your birthday?	It's in November.
	are	your classes?	They're in the morning.

The past tense of *have* is *had*.
*I **had** a headache yesterday.*

Have for Health Problems

We use *have* to talk about health problems.

Affirmative Statements

Subject	*have/has*	Noun
I You	have	a headache.
He She	has	a fever.
We You They	have	colds.

Negative Statements

Subject	*don't/doesn't*	*have/has*	Noun
I You	don't		a headache.
He She	doesn't	have	a fever.
We You They	don't		colds.

The present continuous tense is also called the present progressive tense.

Present Continuous

We use the present continuous tense for actions happening now.

Affirmative Statements

Subject	*be*	Verb + *-ing*	noun
I	am		
You	are		
He She	is	buying	pants.
We They	are		

Negative Statements

Subject	*be + not*	Verb + *-ing*	Noun
I	'm not		
You	aren't		
He She	isn't	buying	a jacket.
We They	aren't		

> The verbs *go* and *do* are irregular with *he/she*. Thomas *goes* to class. Julia *does* her homework.

Simple Present Tense Statements

We use the simple present tense to talk about routines and daily activities.

Affirmative Statements

Subject	Verb
I You	work.
He She	works.
We You They	work.

Negative Statements

Subject	*don't/doesn't*	Verb
I You	don't	work.
He She	doesn't	works.
We You They	don't	work.

Yes/No Questions in the Simple Present Tense

We use *yes/no* questions in the simple present tense to ask about daily activities.

Questions

Do/Does	Subject	Verb	
Do	I you		
Does	he she	work	on Tuesdays?
Do	we you they		

Short Answers

	Subject	*do/does*		Subject	*don't/doesn't*
Yes,	I you	do.	No,	I you	don't.
	he she	does.		he she	doesn't.
	we you	do.		we you they	don't.

Information Questions with *Where, When, What*

Question

Question Word	*do/does*	Subject	Main Verb
Where When What	do	I you	eat?
	does	he she	
	do	we you they	

Short Answers

At Main Street Café.
At 12:30.
Sandwiches and salads.

There is and There are

Affirmative Statements

There	be	Noun	
There	is	a map	in the classroom.
	are	windows	

Negative Statements

There			
There	isn't	a teacher	in the classroom.
	aren't	any windows	

Yes/No Questions

Be	there	Noun
Is	there	a map?
Are		any windows?

Answers

	there	be
Yes,	there	is
		are.

	there	be
No,	there	isn't.
		aren't.

The Simple Past Tense of Be

Was and were are the past tense of be.

Affirmative

Subject	was/were	
I	was	happy.
You	were	
He / She / It	was	on the platform.
We / You / They	were	in Mexico in 1999.

Negative

Subject	was/were + not	
I	was not	sad.
You	were not	
He / She / It	was not	on the bus.
We / You / They	were not	here.

Contractions

was not = wasn't
were not = weren't

Yes/No Questions with the Past Tense of Be

Questions

Was/Were	Subject	
Was	I	late?
Were	you	at a movie?
Was	he / she / it	interesting?
Were	we / you / they	on time?

Short Answers

	Subject	was/were
Yes,	you	were.
	I	was.
	he / she / it	was.
	we / you / they	were.

	Subject	was/were + not
No,	you	weren't.
	I	wasn't.
	he / she / it	wasn't.
	we / you / they	weren't.

Past Tense Statements With Regular Verbs

We often use time expressions with the past tense.

Affirmative Statements

Subject	Verb	Time Expression
I You He She We You They	worked studied moved	last week. yesterday. last night. in 1999.

Negative Statements

Subject	*didn't*	Verb	Time Expression
I You He She We You They	didn't	work study move	last week. yesterday. last night. in 1999.

Irregular Past Tense Verbs

Present		Simple Past	
be	lend	was/were	lent
become	lose	became	lost
begin	make	began	made
break	meet	broke	met
bring	pay	brought	paid
buy	put	bought	put
catch	read	caught	read
choose	ride	chose	rode
come	run	came	ran
cost	say	cost	said
do	see	did	saw
draw	sell	drew	sold
drink	send	drank	sent
drive	shut	drove	shut
eat	sing	ate	sang
fall	sleep	fell	slept
feel	speak	felt	spoke
fight	spend	fought	spent
find	stand	found	stood
fly	steal	flew	stole
forget	swim	forgot	swam
get	take	got	took
give	teach	give	taught
go	tell	went	told
grow	think	grew	thought
have	throw	had	threw
hear	understand	heard	understood
hit	wake	hit	woke
keep	wear	kept	wore
know	win	knew	won
leave	write	left	wrote

Future With *Going To*

We use *be going to* to talk about:
- Future plans. (I'm **going to** get married this summer.)
- Things we can see are going to happen soon. (Look at those clouds! It's **going to** rain.)

Affirmative Statements

Subject	*be*	*going to*	Verb
I	am		
You	are		
He She	is	going to	move.
We You They	are		

Negative Statements

Subject	*be*	*not*	*going to*	Verb
I	am			
You	are			
He She	is	not	going to	move.
We You They	are			

She's not. = She isn't.
We're not. = We aren't.

Questions With *Be Going To*

Questions

be	Subject	*going to*	Verb	
Am	I			
Are	you		paint	the living room?
Is	he she	going to		
Are	we they		rent	the apartment?

Answers

Yes, you are.	No, you're not.
Yes, I am.	No, I'm not.
Yes, he is.	No, he's not.
Yes, she is.	No, she's not.
Yes, we are.	No, we're not.
Yes, they are.	No, they're not.

Can for Ability

We use *can* to talk about ability.

Affirmative/Negative Statements

Subject	can/can't	Verb	
I You He She We You They	can can't	drive use speak	a taxi. a copier. English.

Questions

Can	Subject	Verb
Can	I you he she we they	drive? read?

Answers

Yes/No	Subject	can/can't
Yes,	I you he she we they	can.
No,		can't.

Should for Advice

We use *should* to give advice or say that something is a good idea.

Statements

Subject	should/shouldn't	Verb
I You He She We You They	should shouldn't	rest.

Questions

should	Subject	Verb
Should	I you he she we you they	rest?

Answers

Yes/No	Subject	should/shouldn't
Yes, No,	you I he she we you they	should. shouldn't.

Audioscript

Unit 1

LESSON 2
Activity 3 (page 9)
1. Somalia
2. the United States
3. Mexico
4. Colombia
5. China
6. Cuba

LESSON 3
Pronunciation: Stress in Numbers (page 10)
B.
1. 13
2. 90
3. 50
4. 116
5. 70
6. 4010

Activity 1 (page 10)
1. My address is 1540 Broad Street.
2. My phone number is (305)-555-1723.
3. My school is at 6013 Market Street.

Activity 2 (page 10)
1. *A:* Hi, Mary. Where are you from?
   B: I'm from Colombia.
2. *A:* What is your name, please?
   B: Roberto Ruiz.
   A: What country are you from?
   B: Mexico.
3. *A:* This is Han. She's from Korea.
   B: Hello, Han.

LESSON 5
Activity 5 (page 15)
1. Musa is from Somalia.
2. Luis is from Mexico.
3. Lily is from Vietnam.
4. Ivan is from Russia.

LESSON 6
Activity 1 (page 16)
1. My name is Anna Park.
2. My telephone number is 512-555-7702.
3. My address is 70 Pine Street.
4. My zip code is 20026.
5. I'm single, and I am a police officer.

Unit 2

LESSON 2
Activity 1 (page 24)
1. Nick is **tall**.
2. Ray is **short**.
3. Mike is **heavy**.
4. Liz is **thin**.
5. Sara is **old**.
6. Anna and Kelly are **young**.
7. Tina is **pretty**.
8. Don is **handsome**.

Activity 4 (page 25)
1. Is Berta funny?
2. Is Sam hardworking?
3. Is Kay old?
4. Are Pam and Bob short?

LESSON 3
Activity 1 (page 26)
Conversation 1
A: I think he's funny.
B: Really?
A: Uh-huh. He's thin, too.

Conversation 2
A: Wow. Look. She's tall.
B: And pretty, too.

Conversation 3
A: She's pretty.
B: Who? The heavy one or the thin one?
A: The heavy one.

Conversation 4
A: He isn't tall.
B: But he's handsome.

Pronunciation (page 26)
B.
1. Is he shy?
2. Is she messy?
3. Is she from Mexico?
4. Is he handsome?
5. Is he single?
6. Is she a police officer?

LESSON 6
Activity 2 (page 32)
(phone ringing)
A: Hello?
B: Hi. Is Lucy there?
A: No, she's not. She's at school. May I take a message?
B: Yes, please. This is her brother Jack. I'm here in Boston. Our parents are here, too.
A: What's your phone number?
B: (617)-555-1903.

Activity 3 (page 32)
(phone ringing)
A: Hello?
B: Hello. Is Ben there?
A: No, he's not. May I take a message?
B: Yes, please. This is his aunt Ann.
A: What's your phone number?
B: I'm in New York. It's (212) 555-3064.

Unit 3

LESSON 2
Activity 1 (page 40)
1. There is a pencil.
2. There is a pen.
3. There is a backpack.
4. There is a marker.
5. There is a cell phone.
6. There is a bag.
7. There is a book.
8. There is a notebook

Activity 4 (page 41)
1. How many students are there?
2. How many desks are there?
3. How many notebooks are there?
4. How many maps are there?
5. How many markers are there?
6. How many books are there?
7. How many cell phones are there?
8. How many backpacks are there on the floor?

LESSON 3
Activity 1 (page 42)
1. Is there a meeting room?
2. Are there computer classes?
3. Are there DVDs?
4. Are there books in Spanish?

Activity 2 (page 40)
1. The DVDs are on the shelves.
2. There is a copier in the meeting room.
3. My backpack is on the table.

LESSON 5
Activity 1 (page 42)
The information desk is on the first floor.
The security office is at 521 Fifth Street.
The library is on Fifth Street.
The computer lab is in Room 102.

LESSON 6
Activity 2 (page 48)
Welcome to Washington Adult School and English class. The vending machines are in the snack bar. There are student books in the library. There are restrooms in the main hall.

UNIT 4

LESSON 2
Activity 1 (page 56)
It's cool in the spring.
It's hot in the summer.
It's windy in the fall.
It's cold in the winter.

Activity 5 (page 57)
1. Elizabeth is a student in London. Right now, it's winter. It's cold and foggy.
2. Carlos is in Mexico City. It's winter, but it's warm and sunny.
3. Hong is in Chicago. It's winter. It's cold and windy.
4. Eduardo is in Bogotá. It's summer. It's hot and humid.

LESSON 3
Activities 1 and 2 (page 58)
Here is a look at today's weather. In Miami, it's very sunny. It's hot. It's 98°. In New York, it's not hot. It's only 60°. It's cool, and it's rainy. In Boston, it's 30°. It's cold and snowy.

LESSON 5
Activity 1 (page 62)
1. A. When is New Year's Day?
   B. It's on January 1.
2. A. When is Valentine's Day?
   B. It's on February 14.
3. A. When is Independence Day?
   B. It's on July 4.
4. A. When is Labor Day?
   B. It's in September.
5. A. When is Halloween?
   B. It's on October 31.
6. A. When is Thanksgiving?
   B. It's in November.

Pronunciation (page 62)
B.
1. Today is December 15th.
2. There are 21 students.
3. I am thirty years old.
4. Independence Day is on July 4.
5. I have 12 pencils.
6. It's April 9th.

LESSON 6
Activity 3 (page 64)
Conversation 1
A: Excuse me. When is the first day of class?
B: It's on August 31.

A: And what time is class?
B: 10:00 A.M.
A: Okay. Thank you!

Conversation 2
A: Mr. Brown?
B: Yes?
A: What is the first holiday?
B: It's Labor Day. It's on September 4.
A: Are there classes?
B: No, there aren't. There are no classes.

Conversation 3
[phone conversation]:
A: Ashville Community School, can I help you?
B: Hi. I'm a new student. Is there a new student meeting?
A: Yes, on September 7. At 7:00 P.M.
B: Thanks!

UNIT 5

LESSON 2
Activity 5 (page 73)
1. The hospital is next to the apartment building.
2. The bank is between the drugstore and the post office.
3. The fire station is across from the apartment building.
4. The supermarket is between the community center and the movie theater.

LESSON 3
Activity 1 (page 74)
1. A: Where's the post office?
   B: It's next to the bank.
2. A: Where's the hospital?
   B: It's across from the fire station.
3. A: Where is the school?
   B: It's between the library and the apartment building.

Activity 2 (page 74)
1. A: Where's the supermarket?
   B: It's across from the post office.
2. A: Where is the community center?
   B: It's next to the supermarket.
3. A: Where's the fire station?
   B: It's next to the community center.
4. A: Where's the bank?
   B: It's across from the first station.
5. A: Where is the movie theater?
   B: It's between the post office and the bank.

LESSON 5
Activity 3 (page 79)
Go straight on Broadway. Then . . .
1. Turn left on 6th Avenue. Don't turn right.
2. Don't go on 4th Avenue. It's a one-way street.
3. Do not enter on Sherman Drive.
4. Stop at E Street in front of the apartment building.
5. Don't park on the street. Go behind the apartment building.

LESSON 6
Activity 2 (page 80)
1. Turn right on Princeton Street.
2. Go straight for two blocks.
3. Cross at First Street.
4. Turn left on Fifth Street.
5. Park on the street in front of the house.

UNIT 6

LESSON 2
Activity 1 (page 88)
1. Anita is wearing a white dress and a green hat.
2. Matt is wearing orange shorts and a yellow jacket.
3. Larisa is wearing a red shirt and a blue skirt.
4. Marco is wearing brown pants and black shoes.

Activity 5 (page 89)
1. Brad is wearing red pants.
2. Marta is wearing a purple shirt.
3. Clara is buying white shoes.
4. Ali is waiting for his wife.
5. Paula is helping Marta.
6. Oscar is carrying four bags.

LESSON 3
Activity 1 (page 90)
1. A: Hello. Can I help you?
   B: Yes, I'm looking for pants.
   A: What color?
   B: Brown.
   A: Okay. The brown pants are over there.
   B: Thank you!
2. A: Hello. Can I help you?
   B: Yes, I'm looking for a black skirt.
   A: What size?
   B: Small.
   A: Okay. There are black skirts over there.
   B: Thanks.
3. A: Hello. Can I help you?
   B: Yes, I'm looking for a jacket. A purple jacket.
   A: What size?
   B: Medium.
   A: Okay. The jackets are over there.
   B: Thank you.

B. (page 90)
1. Oscar isn't buying brown pants.
2. Sara and Maria are looking for a black skirt.
3. Mark isn't trying on a blue jacket.
4. They aren't looking for a red shirt.

LESSON 5

Activity 1 (page 94)
1. This shirt is $7.00.
2. That skirt is $10.00.
3. These jackets are $12.00.
4. Those hats are $18.00.

Activity 4 (page 95)
1. *A:* Excuse me. How much is this shirt?
   B: That shirt is $7.00.
   A: There is a problem with my receipt. The total is wrong.
   B: Oh, okay. Your new total is $59.00.
   A: Thanks.
2. *A:* Hi! Please help me.
   B: What is the problem?
   A: There is a problem with my receipt. How much are these pants?
   B: Those pants are $29.
   A: Not $32?
   B: No… Oh, I'm sorry! Your new total is $51.00.
   A: Thank you.
3. *A:* Excuse me. There is a problem with my receipt. How much are these shoes?
   B: They're $35.00.
   A: The total is wrong.
   B: I'm sorry! Your new total is $76.00.
   A: Thanks.

LESSON 6

Activity 2 (page 96)
A: This week, come to Clothes Corner! All our clothes are ON SALE! Shirts, pants, dresses! Shoes, too!
B: How much are the pants?
A: Black pants are on sale! $29!!
B: How much are dresses?
A: There are purple and blue dresses. They're $40!
C: How much are shoes?
A: Brown shoes! Only $35!!
D: How much are shirts?
A: Children's shirts, all colors, are $7!! Don't miss this sale! Come to Clothes Corner today!

UNIT 7

LESSON 2

Activity 5 (page 105)
At 9:00 on Saturday mornings.
1. Luz usually takes a shower at 9:00 A.M.
2. Roberto often cooks breakfast.
3. Miguel always brushes his teeth.
4. Rosa usually gets dressed 9:00 A.M..
5. Jose and Mariela sometimes read books.

LESSON 3

Activity 1 (page 106)
1. Bella always gets up at 7:00 on Wednesdays.
2. Hector often cooks dinner at 7:00.
3. Elisa usually eats breakfast at 10:00 on Saturdays.

Activity 2 (page 106)
Lisa: Hi Elena!
Elena: Oh hi, Lisa. How are you?
Lisa I'm tired . . .
Elena: Why?
Lisa: I'm doing a lot right now . . .
Elena: Like what?
Lisa: Well, I always get up at 6:00 A.M.and shower. After my shower, I eat breakfast with my family, and then I work all day . . . I often work 8 or 10 hours. At night, I usually cook dinner or help my children. I sometimes read. I go to bed at 11 P.M.
Elena: You *are* busy!

LESSON 5

Activity 1 (page 110)
1. *A:* Does Rosa arrive at 9:00 a.m.?
   B: Yes, she does.
2. *A:* Does Alicia take a break at 12:15 p.m.?
   B: No, she doesn't.
3. *A:* Do they leave work at 5:00 p.m.?
   B: No, they don't.
4. *A:* Does she come home at 7:00 p.m.?
   B: Yes, she does.

Pronunciation (page 110)
B.
1. Does she drive a car?
2. Does he go to school?
3. Does she work on Saturdays?
4. Does he ride the bus?

Activity 4 (page 111)
A: Hi, Kristin! How are you?
B: Pretty good, thanks, Mike. I'm very busy these days, though!
A: Oh, really?

B: Yes, I have a new job. I'm a salesclerk at Shoe World. I arrive at work every morning at 8:00 and I leave at 6:00.

A: Huh, that's a long day. Do you take a break?

B: Yes, I take a lunch break at 1:00.

A: That's good.

B: And I take a class in the evening!

A: Really? Do you eat dinner?

B: Yes, I go home and eat dinner at 7:00. My class is at 8:00.

A: You *are* busy!

LESSON 6
Activity 2 (page 112)

1. *A:* Do you work, Bima?
   B: Yes, I do. I work Monday, Tuesday, and Wednesday.
2. *A:* You work a lot, Tony.
   B: Not really. Only Monday, Wednesday, and Friday!
3. *A:* Hong, do you work on Thursday?
   B: Yes, I do. I work on Tuesday, Wednesday, and Thursday.
4. *A:* John, you work too much.
   B: You're right. I work on Tuesday, Thursday, Friday, and Saturday.

Unit 8

LESSON 2
Activity 1 (page 120)

1. a loaf of bread
2. a carton of milk
3. a bag of carrots
4. a box of cereal
5. a bottle of juice
6. a pound of fish

Activity 5 (page 121)

1. How much are the bananas?
2. How much is the coffee?
3. How much are the apples?
4. How much are the onions?

LESSON 3
Pronunciation
B. (page 122)

1. live
2. meat
3. eat
4. cheap
5. sit
6. chick

Activity 1 (page 122)
Conversation 1:

A: Let's buy apples. They're on sale.

B: How much are they?

A: $3 a bag.

Conversation 2:

A: Let's buy some orange juice. It's on sale.

B: How much is it?

A: $2.50 a bottle.

Conversation 3:

A: The chicken is on sale.

B: How much is it?

A: $1.29 a pound.

Conversation 4:

A: Bread is a good price.

B: How much is it?

A: $2.15 a loaf.

LESSON 5
Activity 1 (page 126)

1. They have milk.
2. They need water.
3. They want eggs.

LESSON 6
Activity 2 (page 128)

Waiter: Hello. What would you like today?

Female: Hmm. I'll have a hamburger, please.

Waiter: Would you like French fries or chips with that?

Female: I'll have chips, please.

Waiter: Any soup?

Female: Oh, no thank you, but maybe dessert….

Waiter: We have ice cream and pie.

Female: The ice cream, please.

Waiter: And something to drink?

Female: Yes, a small milk, please.

Waiter: Of course. So, that's a hamburger with chips, ice cream, and a small milk.

Female: Yes, thank you.

UNIT 9

LESSON 2
Activity 1 (page 136)

1. A plumber can fix toilets.
2. An accountant can use a calculator.
3. An electrician can fix wiring.
4. A mechanic can fix trucks.

Activity 5 (page 137)
1. Kathy and Jake can make lunch.
2. Andy can't lift the box.
3. Ana can fix water pipes.
4. Trung can take blood pressure.
5. Greg can't fix the car.
6. Yuri can drive an ambulance.

LESSON 3
Activity 1 (page 138)
1. Welcome to Jobline. Please listen for available openings. There is an opening for an office assistant, position number A112. This person needs to use a computer and other office equipment.
2. Welcome to Jobline. Please listen for available openings. There are two openings for a sales person, position number G801. The position requires phone skills in English and Spanish.
3. Welcome to Jobline. Please listen for available openings. There is one opening for a mechanic, position number T99. Applicants must be able to fix cars and trucks.

Pronunciation (page 138)
B.
1. I can cook Japanese food.
2. She can't fix the toilet.
3. You can't drive a bus.

LESSON 6
Activity 4 (page 144)
1. In my last job, I used the cash register and served customers at a restaurant.
2. In my last job, I used a computer and answered the phone.
3. I can fix anything. I worked at a small company. I fixed electrical problems.
4. I need a job. I can cook all types of food. In my last job, I worked at a hospital. I made salads and cooked meals.

Unit 10

LESSON 2
Activity 1 (page 152)
1. Three students were early yesterday.
2. Four students were on time yesterday.
3. One student was late.
4. The classroom was crowded at 11:00.
5. The classroom was empty last night.
6. The students were noisy yesterday.
7. The teacher was quiet this morning.

Activity 5 (page 153)
1. The airport was empty.
2. The flight was noisy.
3. The train was crowded.
4. The street was noisy.

LESSON 3
Activity 1 (page 154)
Hi Patricia, this is Liza. I'm calling from the bus station in Orlando. The weather is terrible. My bus from Atlanta was late, so I didn't get the 1:45 bus to Miami. Now, I'm getting on the 3:15 bus. Can you pick me up at the Miami bus station?

Pronunciation (page 154)
B.
1. *A:* Is the train here?
   B: Uh-huh. It's on Platform 2.
2. *A:* Is the bus here?
   B: Unh-uh. The bus comes at 4:00. It's only 3:30.
3. *A:* The meeting started at 9:00.
   B: Uh-oh. We're late.
4. *A:* Is the meeting over?.
   B: Uh-huh. It's time for lunch.
5. *A:* Oh, no! I missed my bus!

LESSON 5
Activity 1 (page 158)
1. The traffic was slow.
2. The roads were dangerous.
3. The mountains were beautiful.
4. The boat was fast.
5. The lake was clean.
6. The hotel was dirty.

LESSON 6
Activity 2 (page 160)
A: How was your vacation, Susan?
B: Okay, I guess.
A: Did you go to the mountains?
B: No, I was at the beach in San Fernandina.
A: How was the weather?
B: It was warm and rainy. But the hotel was really nice. My room was large and clean. It was a little noisy, though.
A: How did you get there?
B: By bus. Unfortunately, the bus was really slow and dirty.

UNIT 11

LESSON 2
Activity 1 (page 168)
1. Samira's back hurts.
2. Antonio's head and neck hurt.
3. Eva's stomach hurts.
4. Ramon's ear hurts.
5. Rosa's hands and arms hurt.
6. Joe's legs and feet hurt.

Activity 4 (page 169)
1. Elena has a backache.
2. Eliza's ears hurt.
3. Alex has a stomachache.
4. Gloria's nose hurts.
5. Luis has a headache.
6. Ibrahim has a cold.

LESSON 3
Activity 1 (page 170)
1. *A:* Hi Elga! Are you okay?
   B: Not really. I have a really bad stomachache. My head hurts too… I think I have the flu.
   A: I'm sorry!
2. *A:* Jung, are you okay?
   B [*with mixed emotions*]: I'm okay… my whole family is sick.
   A: I'm sorry to hear that!
   B: Yeah. We all have colds. We all have coughs and our throats hurt a lot. Our ears hurt a lot too, and we have headaches.
3. *A:* Richard, what's wrong?
   B: Ooohhh… my back really hurts! I was in a car accident last weekend. My head hurts, too.
   A: Oh no – I'm sorry! Call a doctor!

Activity 2 (page 171)
1.
A: AAA Construction Company.
B Mrs. Green? Hi, this is Radek.
A: Oh hi, Radek! Are you okay?
B: Not really. I have the flu. I can't come to work today.
A: Oh, that's too bad!
B: Can you tell Mr. Howard for me?
A: Sure.

2.
Please leave a message after the tone. (BEEP) Hi, Mr. Brown. This is Patricia. I can't work today . I have a cold and a bad headache. Can Isaac work instead? Thanks. (BEEP). [automated voice: "Monday, September 4, 10:24 A.M."}

3.
A: Hi, Maria? This is Audrey. I know it's 9:30 already, but I can't come to work today.
B: Oh no! Why not?
A: I have a terrible backache.
B: Oh, I'm sorry.
A: I can't even walk!
B: Oh, how awful!
A: Can you tell Mrs. Smith?
A: Yes, sure. Thanks for calling. Get better soon!

LESSON 5
Activity 1 (page 174)
1. Mark has a cold.
   He should take cough medicine.
2. Musa has an earache.
   He should use ear drops.
3. Ellen's head hurts.
   She should take a pain reliever.
4. Tina has a sore throat.
   She should take a throat lozenge.

Pronunciation (page 174)
B.
1. Marco shouldn't call 911.
2. Henry should take cough medicine.
3. Sara should stay in bed.
4. Gloria should use ear drops.

LESSON 6
Activity 2 (page 176)
A: Centerville Family Practice. Can I help you?
B: Hi, I need to make an appointment.
A: Are you a new patient?
B: Yes, I am.
A: Okay. There is an appointment on Friday, July 28th with Dr. Lopez.
B: Great! What time?
A: 1:45 P.M.
B: Okay.
A: What is your name?
B: Carlos Rodriguez.
A: And your phone number?
B: 973-1265.
A: What is your insurance?
B: Excellent Health Insurance. The policy number is 108407.
A: What is the reason for your visit?
B: I have a stomachache and a fever.
A: Okay. For the appointment, you should bring your insurance card. You should arrive 15 minutes early.
B: Okay. Thank you!
A: You're welcome. See you on Friday.

UNIT 12

LESSON 3

Activity 1 (page 186)
A: Good news, Mark!
B: What?
A: James and Linda are going to get married!
B: That's great! When?
A: Next month.
B: Wow! So… what are they going to do after the wedding?
A: Well, first, they're going to California for their honeymoon. Then they're going to move.
B: Oh really?
A: Yeah. After they move, Linda's going to start a new job.
B: Huh. What's James going to do?
A: He's going to sell his car to save money. This fall, he's going to go back to school.
B: That's great!

LESSON 5

Activity 1 (page 190)
living room
kitchen
dining room
bedroom
bathroom

Activity 3 (page 190)
A: Hi, Mr. Smith? This is Linda Herrera.
B: Oh hi, Linda. How can I help you?
A: [*friendly, but a little testy*]: Well, I'm calling about some problems in our apartment.
B: Um….. Can you tell me again what the problems are?
A: Well, the toilet is broken.
B: Oh, I'm going to fix the toilet.
A: Oh, good. And the stairs aren't safe.
B: Okay. Well, the carpenters are going to fix the stairs.
A: All right. And what about the cabinets in the living room?
B: Oh… right. The carpenters can fix those, too.
A: Okay. Thanks. Oh, and can you fix the window in the bedroom?
B: Oh, yes, yes…
A: By the way, we're going to paint the dining room white. Is that okay?
B: Yes, sure.
A: Okay. Thanks again! See you tomorrow?
B: Um…. Yes…. Tomorrow!

LESSON 6

Activity 2 (page 192)
A: Hi Paula! How are you?
B: Fine. I'm looking for a new place to live.
A: Great! Is there anything good?
B: Well, I think I'm going to rent a little house. It has three bedrooms and two bathrooms!
A: Wow!
B: Yes, it's exciting, but it has a lot of problems….
A: Oh no! Like what?
B: Well, the kitchen cabinets are very old, and I don't like the paint color. And the dishwasher doesn't work either.
A: Oh, that's too bad.
B: It's okay. The carpet isn't clean either, but I'm going to call someone to clean it. It's going to be very nice soon.
B: Good luck!
A: Thanks!

Vocabulary

Numbers in parentheses indicate unit numbers.

accountant (9)
across from (6)
actor (1)
address (1)
afternoon (4)
airplane (10)
airport (10)
always (7)
amusement park (10)
answer (9)
apartment building (5)
apple (8)
appointment (11)
April (4)
arrive (7)
ask (9)
August (4)
aunt (2)
baby (12)
back (11)
backache (10)
backpack (3)
badge number (1)
bag (3)
baggage claim (10)
banana (8)
bandage (11)
bank (5)
bathroom (12)
beach (10)
beautiful (10)
bed (7)
bedroom (12)
behind (6)
between (6)
black (6)
block (5)
blood pressure (9)
blue (6)
board (3)
book (3)
boring (10)
borrow (9)
bottle (8)
box (8)
Brazil (1)
bread (8)
break/broke (9)
broccoli (8)
brother (2)
brown (6)
brush (7)
bus (10)
bus stop (10)
buy (6)

cabinets (12)
cable television (12)
calculator (9)
call (7)
Canada (1)
car (9)
carpenter (9)
carpet (12)
carrot (8)
carry (6)
carton (8)
CDs (3)
cell phone (3)
cent (6)
cereal (8)
chair (3)
cheese (8)
cheeseburger (8)
chicken (8)
child (1)
children (1)
China (1)
city (12)
clean (7)
clear (4)
clock (3)
close (9)
cloudy (4)
coffee (8)
cold (4)
Colombia (1)
come (9)
community center (5)
computer (3)
computer lab (3)
construction worker (1)
cook (1)
cool (4)
copier (3)
cough (10)
count (9)
cousins (2)
cross (5)
crowded (10)
Cuba (1)
dairy products (8)
dangerous (10)
daughter (2)
December (4)
deliver (9)
dentist (1)
desk (3)
dessert (8)
dime (6)
dining room (12)

dirty (10)
dishwasher (12)
doctor (1)
dollar (6)
dress (6)
dresser (12)
drink (11)
drive (7)
drugstore (5)
DVD (3)
ear (11)
early (10)
eat (7)
egg (8)
electrician (9)
elevator (3)
email address (1)
empty (10)
enter (5)
evening (4)
excellent (10)
exciting (10)
exercise (11)
experience (9)
extra large (6)
extra small (6)
fall (4)
fast (10)
father (2)
February (4)
feet (11)
female (1)
fever (10)
finish (12)
fire station (5)
first name (1)
fish (8)
fix (9)
flu (10)
foggy (4)
forklift (9)
French fries (8)
Friday (7)
fruit (8)
full-time (9)
fun (10)
funny (2)
garage
gas station (5)
gate (10)
gender (1)
get dressed (7)
get married (12)
get up (7)
go (5)

good (10)
grain (8)
grandfather (2)
grandmother (2)
green (6)
hall (3)
Halloween (4)
hamburgers (8)
hand (11)
handsome (2)
hardworking (2)
hat (6)
have/has (11)
headache (10)
heating pad (11)
heavy (2)
help (6)
homework (7)
hospital (5)
hot (4)
hot dogs (8)
hotel (5)
house (5)
housekeeper (1)
humid (4)
hurt (11)
husband (2)
ice (11)
ice cream (8)
iced tea (8)
in front of (3)
Independence Day (4)
information (9)
install (12)
interesting (10)
Internet access (12)
jacket (6)
January (4)
juice (8)
July (4)
June (4)
kitchen (12)
Korea (1)
Labor Day (4)
lake (10)
large (6)
last name (1)
late (10)
lazy (2)
leave (7)
left turn (5)
library (3)
listen (8)
living room (12)
loaf (8)

lobby (3)
look (6)
made (9)
make (5)
male (1)
man (1)
map (3)
March (4)
marker (3)
married (1)
May (4)
measure (9)
measurement (9)
meat (8)
mechanic (9)
medicine (11)
medium (6)
meeting room (3)
men (1)
messy (2)
Mexico (1)
microwave (12)
milk (8)
Monday (7)
morning (4)
mother (2)
mountain (10)
move (9)
movie (10)
movie theater (5)
museum (10)
neat (2)
neck (11)
never (7)
New Year's Day (4)
next to (5)
nickel (6)
night (4)
noisy (10)
notebook (3)
November (4)
nurse (1)
occupation (1)
October (4)
office (3)
office assistant (1)
old (2)
on time (10)
one (6)
one-way (5)
onion (8)
open (9)
orange (6)
orange (8)
order (9)

organize (9)
outgoing (2)
pack
paint (9)
pants (6)
park (5)
parking (5)
part-time (9)
patient (9)
pay (12)
pen (3)
pencil (3)
pencil sharpener (3)
penny (6)
people (1)
person (1)
phone company (12)
pie (8)
platform (10)
play (7)
plumber (9)
police officer (1)
police station (5)
post office (5)
potato chips (8)
pound (8)
prescription (11)
pretty (2)
public telephone (3)
purple (6)
put (11)
quarter (6)
quiet (10)
rainy (4)
read (7)
receive (9)
red (6)
refrigerator (8)
relaxing (10)
rent (12)
rest (11)
restaurant (5)
restroom (3)
rice (8)
ride (7)
right turn (5)
runny nose (10)
Russia (1)
safe
salad (8)
salesclerk (1)
sandwich (8)
Saturday (7)
scanner (9)
scary (10)

school (3)
security office (3)
sell (12)
September (4)
serious (2)
server (1)
shelf (9)
shirt (6)
shoes (6)
shop (6)
short (2)
shorts (6)
shy (2)
sick (10)
single (1)
sister (2)
skirt (6)
slow (10)
small (6)
snack bar (3)
snowy (4)
Social Security number (1)
soda (8)
sofa (12)
Somalia (1)
sometimes (7)
son (2)
sore throat (10)
soup (8)
speak (9)
spring (4)
stairs (3)
start (5)
stay (11)
stomach (11)
stomachache (10)
stop (5)
straight (5)
stressful (10)
students (1)
study (7)
summer (4)
Sunday (7)
sunny (4)
supermarket (5)
supervise (9)
table (3)
take (7)
take a break (7)
take a class (7)
talk (6)
tall (2)
taxi driver (1)
teacher (1)

telephone number (1)
terrible (10)
Thanksgiving (4)
that (6)
The United States (1)
these (6)
thin (2)
this (6)
those (6)
throat (11)
Thursday (7)
ticket counter (10)
toilet (9)
train (10)
train station (10)
trash can (3)
truck (9)
try on (6)
Tuesday (7)
turn (5)
twenty (3)
uncle (2)
use (9)
usually (7)
U-turn (5)
Valentine's Day (4)
vegetables (8)
vending machine (3)
Vietnam (8)
visit (9)
wait (6)
walk (7)
wall (12)
warm (4)
wash (9)
watch (7)
water fountain (3)
Wednesday (7)
went (9)
white (6)
wife (2)
window (3)
windy (4)
winter (4)
wiring (9)
woman (1)
women (1)
work (6)
worker (9)
x-ray (9)
yellow (6)
yogurt (8)
young (2)
zip code (1)

Index

Academic Skills

GRAMMAR

GRAPHS, CHARTS, MAPS

LISTENING

MATH

PRONUNCIATION

READING

Career Skills

Life Skills

CONSUMER EDUCATION

Buying and selling, 86, 87, 91, 93, 97, 98, 120

Calculating prices, expenses, wages, 95, 97, 100, 112

Checks, 96, 97

Clothing, clothing sizes, 88, 90, 91, 93, 95, 96, 97

Food, 118-132

Hours of operation, 128

Household repairs, 193

Labels, signs, 48, 78, 175

Prices, buying and selling, 86, 87, 91-100, 120-123

Weights and Measures, 31, 58, 121, 127,132

ENVIRONMENT AND WORLD

Building Map, 3.60

Campus Map, 49

City Maps, 74, 79, 80

Countries, 8, 9, 10, 11, 15, 18, 130

United States Map, 4.21

Weather and Seasons, 54-57, 59, 63, 162, 163

World Map, 9

FAMILY AND PARENTING

Clothing, sizes, 88, 90-93, 96-99

Food, 118-132

Health problems, remedies, 166-179

Housing, 28-35, 114, 190

Routine activities, 103, 104, 105, 106, 107, 108, 109, 110, 111, 113, 115, 123, 124, 126

GOVERNMENT AND COMMUNITY

Educational opportunities, 84, 116

Government services, 83

Identification, 20

Jobs line, 138

Library, 42, 43

Medical services, 176, 177

Places in the Community, 70-75, 77, 80-83, 123, 124, 128, 156

Public service occupations, 12, 72

School, 44, 45, 48, 49, 50, 64

Traffic Signs, 78

Resources

Government services, 83

Jobs line, 138

Library, 42, 43

School, 44, 45, 48, 49, 50, 84

HEALTH AND NUTRITION

Doctor, 176, 177

Food, 118-123, 126-132

Health problems, remedies, 166-178

INTERPERSONAL COMMUNICATION

Advice, 172-177

Apologizing, 155

Appointments, 176

Asking for help, 186

Email, 66, 67, 159, 168

Family members, 28-35, 114

Giving directions, 45, 46, 49, 70-81, 83

Introductions, 11

Personal Information, 6-8

Scheduling, 64, 65, 106, 108, 110, 111, 113, 115, 116, 176

Telephone skills, 32, 33, 170, 180

SAFETY AND SECURITY

Dangerous conditions, weather, 162, 163

Emergency procedures, 164

Household repairs, 190-193

Traffic signs, 78

TELEPHONE COMMUNICATION

Appointment, making, 76

Giving telephone number, 6

Jobs line, calling, 138

Messages, 32, 154, 170, 171, 176, 180

TIME AND MONEY

Bus schedule, 154

Calculating expenses, wages, 100, 112, 143

Calendar, 64, 65

Checks, 96, 97

Dates, 32, 33, 64, 176

Future, 182-196

Holidays, 62, 64, 68

Months, 56, 62, 64

Prices, 122, 123, 128

Sales, 98

Schedules, 104,106, 107-113, 116, 159, 176, 184, 185

Seasons, 56, 57, 66

Time, 32, 33, 60, 63, 64, 115

U.S. coins and bills, money, 92-95, 97, 99, 121

TRANSPORTATION AND TRAVEL

Directions, giving and following, 45, 70, 72, 75-83

Maps, 48, 74, 80

Schedue, bus, 154

Schedule, train, 159

Traffic signs, 78

Types, 150

Vacation, 159-163

Topics

Calendar, 64, 65

Clothing, 88, 90-99

Colors, 88, 90, 91

Community, 70-83

Directions and locations, 45, 70-81, 84, 122-124, 156, 193

Education, 3, 48, 49, 50, 84, 116

Family, 28-35, 114

Food, 118-132

Furniture, appliances, 189-193

Future, 182-196

Health problems, remedies, 166-179

Holidays, 62, 68

Housing, landlord,189-193

Letters and Numbers, 2, 123

Measurement, 31, 121

Personal characteristics, 22-27

Personal information, 6-20

Routine activities, 103-111, 115, 116, 124, 126

Shopping, money, 86, 87, 90-100, 120-123, 126, 143

Telephone skills, 32, 33, 180

Time, 60, 64, 110, 111, 113, 115, 154, 159, 176

Travel, 78, 150, 151, 154, 155, 159-163

Weather and Seasons, 54-57, 59, 66, 162-164

Workplace, 2, 36, 52, 68, 72, 84, 112, 113, 132, 134-136, 140, 142, 143, 146-148, 164, 170, 180, 189, 190, 196

Credits